W9-BYK-500

IPADS® IN THE LIBRARY

IPADS® IN THE LIBRARY

Using Tablet Technology to Enhance Programs for All Ages

Joel A. Nichols

AN IMPRINT OF ABC-CLIO, LLC
Santa Barbara, California • Denver, Colorado • Oxford, England

PRO 025.5 NIC
Nichols, Joel A.   iPads in the library : using tablet techn

T 12047

Copyright 2013 by Joel A. Nichols

All rights reserved. No part of this publication may be reproduced, stored in a retrieval
system, or transmitted, in any form or by any means, electronic, mechanical,
photocopying, recording, or otherwise, except for the inclusion of brief quotations in a
review, without prior permission in writing from the publisher.

Library of Congress Cataloging-in-Publication Data

Nichols, Joel A.
  iPads in the library : using tablet technology to enhance programs for all ages / Joel A. Nichols.
    pages cm
  Includes bibliographical references and index.
    ISBN 978–1–61069–347–9 (hard copy) — ISBN 978–1–61069–348–6 (ebook) 1. Libraries—Activity
programs. 2. Multimedia library services. 3. iPad (Computer) 4. Tablet computers. 5. Application
software—Directories. I. Title.
  Z716.33.N527   2013
  025.50285—dc23   2013007684

ISBN: 978–1–61069–347–9
EISBN: 978–1–61069–348–6

17 16 15 14 13   2 3 4 5

This book is also available on the World Wide Web as an eBook.
Visit www.abc-clio.com for details.

Libraries Unlimited
An Imprint of ABC-CLIO, LLC

ABC-CLIO, LLC
130 Cremona Drive, P.O. Box 1911
Santa Barbara, California 93116-1911

This book is printed on acid-free paper ∞

Manufactured in the United States of America

This book is dedicated to my mother, Joanne Beriau Nichols,
whose crafty inspiration and commitment to education brought me here.

Contents

Acknowledgments

Thanks to my family, especially my partner, Ray, for his support in completing this project. Thanks, too, to my many colleagues at the Free Library of Philadelphia who supported this book with lots of brainstorms and encouragement.

Introduction:
Why iPads in the Library?

Library work takes a diverse set of skills working together in unique combinations, and the iPad makes an excellent flexible and robust companion for many kinds of information work. Librarians have often adopted new technological innovations before their patrons, especially when those technologies strengthen and enhance access to information. But the low-cost, highly attractive, and popular eReader and tablet computer world— Kindles, Nooks, Nexus, Galaxy Tabs, iPads, Surfaces—are huge hits with consumers, and in this technology, libraries are not as far ahead as we should be. In addition, most of these devices are designed and optimized for individuals to use in very personal ways.

Even more challenging for libraries used to upgrading to the latest versions of Windows on networked, desktop computers, most of these the tablets and eReaders popular among library patrons are powered either by Apple's closed operating system for its mobile devices, iOS; or by a version of Android, an operating system developed by Google and used by a variety of third-party manufacturers. Microsoft released its long-awaited tablet, the Microsoft Surface, on February 9, 2013.

In addition, these devices use Wi-Fi or LTE (or both) communication signals and, because they are meant to be carried around, tossed in a backpack, stored in a desk drawer, and even go outside, they cannot be networked the way we are used to. Quite literally, our IT staff has not been trained for this. Nonetheless, iPads are already outselling desktop PCs.[1]

So far, these devices are probably not robust enough to replace desktop computers immediately, but they do offer innovative ways to practice reference services and interact with patrons. And as programming tools, tablets—and iPads in particular—are potentially revolutionary.

There are six compelling arguments for iPads in public and school libraries:

1. *Flexibility.* Tablets are just computers: hardware running various software applications. They are tools to deliver and manage digital information, and although the Android Marketplace

and the Apple's iTunes App Store claim similar numbers of available apps for sale, the fragmentation of various Android versions running on hardware manufactured by so many different companies means that for any individual Android device, there are fewer applications, or apps, available. Not all versions of Android run on all devices, and because so many different companies make hardware for the Android operating system, there is little or no standardization. And while Apple's rigid control over which apps are approved and how these apps interact with their hardware rightly earn it an "evil empire" reputation, the end product is a robust hardware tool with intuitive apps that interact with each other fairly seamlessly and an enormous selection of apps developed by third-party designers that make your iPad infinitely versatile.

2. *Ease of use.* Although tablets are similar to desktop computers—hardware that runs various software programs—the fact that they do not use keyboards and mice means that they are much less conceptual. Users can interact with digital objects almost like they do with physical ones, touching and moving them with their fingers, tapping and/or pressing down to select and navigate menus that are usually much simpler and have fewer options that traditional PC menus. Using these devices is intuitive because of the ways in which they replicate real-world physics with animations and screens that rotate and resize automatically. I have seen everyone, from very young children to seniors to adults with different levels of literacy, dexterity, and mobility, start using them proficiently within a few minutes, particularly if they are already inside a given app. (They can be challenging for people with very low levels of literacy, though.)

[Handwritten note in left margin: " Not sure I agree" with arrow pointing to item 2]*

3. *iPads—and other tablets—are books.* Digital books are in libraries and here to stay. These devices represent powerful technologies to deliver books and other textual and visual information on the market. Libraries should have the best and most robust book technologies available. This is the same reason children's librarians buy reinforced hardcover editions.

[Handwritten note in left margin: "Do agree" with arrow pointing to item 3]

4. *Relative affordability.* iPads are not cheap, often costing hundreds of dollars more than the cheaper Android tablets. But compared against Android tablets, netbooks, and ultrabooks with similar hardware capabilities, they are exactly competitive. For libraries used to buying expensive, 15-inch business-class laptops, iPads are a much cheaper option. Libraries struggling to maintain creaking public PCs probably cannot afford an iPad lab, but purchasing one for roving reference or eBook demos, or pursuing cheaper iPod Touches, which also run iOS, to energize programming might just be a friends' group fund-raiser away.

5. *iOS and hardware integration.* The rigid control on Apple's part of limited third-party hardware manufacturers described above also means that librarians are assured that any app from the iTunes store will work on any iOS device. The hardware is designed to interact smoothly with the operating system, and it shows in how intuitive and integrated the design is. See below for additional information about the negative aspects of this rigidity.

6. *Popularity and attractiveness to patrons.* Libraries will buy and use iPads for the same reasons they buy thousands of copies of *50 Shades of Grey* and lend DVDs: patrons want them. Apple's astronomical advertising budget means that nearly everyone has seen iPad commercials and magazine ads even if they have not seen one up close. Patrons, especially young ones, are enthusiastic about using iPads. Even if their excitement comes from the fact that it is a trendy lifestyle product, libraries can leverage this excitement into larger programming audiences and more satisfied and happy users.

Think of the iPad as the Swiss Army knife of tablet computers: high-resolution display, two cameras capable of capturing High Definition (HD) images, a microphone and speakers for effective recording and playback, and Wi-Fi or LTE (3G or 4G wireless signals that connect cellular phones) capability depending on the model. The built-in accelerometer allows the display to rotate, and for apps where you shake the device to clear the screen, use the whole device to control a steering or flying game, or even to serve as a digital carpenter's level. App designers leverage these various hardware parts to make innovative and useful software applications that perform any number of functions with many kinds of data.

On the negative side, iPads suffer from limited file interoperability. For example, when Apple's photo roll app (a native app that is standard to the iPad and cannot be deleted) offers options to email photos as an attachment, print or tweet them, but not to upload them to Facebook. This is a corporate choice, not a limitation in hardware or software. Famously, iOS devices do not support Adobe Flash, which is still the underlying code for many websites. These websites simply do not load on iPads. Increasingly, HTML5 is replacing Flash, but there are still thousands if not millions of webpages and online tools coded in Flash. But many of these frustrations are mitigated by the flexibility of this platform. There are many workarounds for file conversion, and additional apps to perform very specific functions on files. While a motivated user can usually "make it work," something might take five steps rather than just one right-click, as on a PC.

Working with iPads and other tablet computers require flexibility and creative workarounds between file types, connector ports, and operating systems. Because the nature of library and information work is itself adaptable and dynamic, tablet computers are powerful tools to help librarians deliver high-quality programming. Be sure to investigate carefully the limitations and capabilities of the iPads and other tablet computers you are interested in employing in the library, and have a plan for integrating them into your other IT services.

HOW TO USE THIS BOOK

This is a book of library program ideas that incorporate tablet technology. I have conducted these programs using iPads and apps specific to the iTunes Store, but the programs can be done with other tablets as well. See the following section, "Adapting for Other Tablets," for more information about adapting these programs for other devices, apps, and operating systems. Each program plan is structured with goals, apps, planning notes, other required and optional books and materials, and step-by-step instructions. App names appear in bold text to make them easy to recognize. Here is how you might approach the text.

Goal

The library programs outlined in this book each have particular learning goals and interact with specific kinds of literacy and literacy skills. Use this initial description to decide when and how to use this program, as well as a way to justifying the ways in which this program supports other classroom or education standards as well as literacy targets (including multiple literacies and transliteracy). In addition, the outlined goal is a jumping-off point for you to adapt these programs to fit your community, school, or library programming needs. The goal of each program plan shows succinctly what the program offers participants; what participants will produce, if anything; and what skills they will practice and develop.

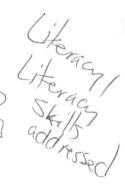

Apps

Each program plan included lists the required apps. Any book about a digital device and its software programs is hindered by the speed with which these apps, as well as iOS, changes. Most of this book was researched and written with iOS 5.11, and while iOS 6 has come out just in time for final revisions, it is impossible to completely prepare for what iOS you might be using by the time the book is actually in your hands or loaded on your iPad. Some of you might already have iOS 7 (or 6.x, or whatever) at that point, and some of you early adopters might have decided to stick with iOS 5.11 or earlier, depending on which model iPad you are using. As the operating system changes, apps themselves must release new versions to keep up. Some do, some do not. Some apps are clearly labeled that they need a particular version of iOS to work, while many will work on several different versions.

With the exception of the preloaded apps and the major Apple ones—**Pages, Keynote, GarageBand, iMovie,** etc.—all of the apps detailed and researched in this book are produced and marketed by third-party companies. Anything could happen with these companies: FingerSketch might go bankrupt and not have the resources to update their code for a new version of iOS. Apple might have a corporate falling out with another company—or Google might buy one of these other software companies—and Apple will remove the particular app from the App Store. Whenever possible, use the apps suggested here. These program plans are all tested with the specific apps described, but based on your budget and the uncontrollable landscape of the App Store, it may be necessary to find alternative apps. Realize, too, that they might change names, be bought or sold to different companies, or repackaged with different graphics and names. With so many apps, chances are you will find an acceptable substitute with a little hunting and testing.

Planning Notes

This section helps you plan for introducing these programs to audiences. It will contain information about setup for the programs, what content to have ready to share, and what in-app work you have to do before the program begins, such as making a sample project or queuing up examples.

Books/Other Materials

In this section, you will find additional materials that may be useful in the program. The materials are often items such as scratch paper, generic art supplies, and headphones but may also include things such as specific objects to photograph. In many ways, lots of the suggested materials are optional, and you can run a program without them. But centrally, to present the strongest programs that address transliteracy and multiple literacies, having analogue creation tools (i.e., craft supplies, paper, clay, etc.) that participants can use alongside the digital ones is essential. Always have pencils, pens, and scratch paper. Also, if possible, have a laptop available in case you hit a dead end with a file format or social media sharing links, or need or want to add in a web tool that uses Adobe Flash.

Step-by-Step Instructions

While the iPad itself and many apps are intuitive and simple to use, it is sometimes necessary to spend significant time teaching yourself apps, how they work and what they can do, as well as troubleshooting the projects described in this book. Many apps have excellent in-app or YouTube tutorials linked from within the app, and there are often interactive help screens to demonstrate specific or particular gestures used in the apps. I have attempted to elucidate any app functions that are not all that intuitive or clear, as well as offer enough structure so that a total beginner can walk themselves through these projects step by step.

Keep in mind that most apps have the same kinds of navigation: there is usually a home/welcome or menu screen, there is usually a project screen or workspace, and there are usually saving and exporting options. In addition, remember that a new version of any of these apps could come out at any time, changing the size or shape of an icon, adding more social media links inside the app, or even radically expanding the functionality. Be sure to leave yourself time to get acquainted with the apps in addition to following the step-by-step instructions. More advanced users should scan for expert hints and tips that were uncovered while using and testing these apps.

Other Sources of Help

If you are having a problem, try a very specific Google search to resolve it. Formulate as specific a question as possible, such as "how to export video **iMovie** to mp4 format" or "**Stitcher** app volume control headphones." It can be useful, as in the former example, to add the words "iPad," "iOS" or "App" to these queries to narrow results, especially if the app has a generic name. Other examples include "Splice iPad app how to trim video" or "**WhirlyGlobe** app turning on/off state labels." These queries will often lead to support forums where many other users detail hours of troubleshooting.

In addition, search for YouTube examples of these apps in action. You might find reviews or tutorials. Construct a YouTube query such as "**LetterTracerHD** app animation" or "Snapseed app tutorial." With better-known apps, try omitting "app" in the query.

Adapting for Other Tablets

Most of these programs can be successfully adapted for smartphones or tablets other than Apple's family of iOS devices (iPad, iPad mini, iPod Touch). Crucial would be the same or similar hardware: Wi-Fi capability or an LTE connection, camera(s) and microphone (including video capture), multitouch interfaces, and so on. Many Android tablets have these same capabilities and are as flexible and sometimes as easy to use.

The second hurdle in adapting to other devices is the software. These are all tested with apps from the iOS app store. In addition to the fragmentation of the Android app platform (not all apps work the same way or at all on all the tablets and devices), Google Play (the Android app store) does not always have a version of the same app. Many major software providers have created Android app versions, including major ones like **Facebook**, **Flipboard**, or **Netflix**.

In addition, there might be very similar apps developed by different companies. For example, an Android app to replace **Felt Board** or **Toontastic** could be something called Storyboard by Jade Publishing. But it is an entirely different app—unique content, unique interface, etc.—so you will have to test and adapt in case the app does not have all the functionality required by one of the programs below.

Adapting for Varying Numbers of iPads

In a perfect world, librarians and teachers would have as many or more iPads as there were students. However, the world is not perfect, and quite likely you will not have that many. Still, most of these programs will work best if there are at least two iPads the participants can use, and one you can use to demonstrate. Most participants can work very well together on these devices. Be sure to structure this sharing among very young users, which might mean clearly identifying roles at the beginning of the program.

Many of the following programs that include video projects, narrated slideshows, comic strips, song making, interactive story creation, etc., will work well with groups up to four or five. For projects planned as an individual activity—for example the Illustrated Acrostic, Crafter's Portfolio or Animated Name Video—consider making substitutions and adaptations such as asking the crafters to design a group portfolio or catalog instead of one just for their own work, or having the animated name be your library, school, or town name instead of a personal name. These changes will depersonalize these projects and make it easier to work with fewer devices and larger groups.

Substituting Apps

The best way to be sure an alternative app will work is to download and test it, whether an Android app on a different device or another app from the iTunes store. Search for alternative apps with the same keywords, and look in the same or analogous categories in each store. Occasionally, searching the web with queries such as "Android alternative to **GarageBand**" or "Free alternative to **Keynote** iPad app" may also return useful results.

PROGRAM SERIES

The programs in this book are organized by audience age groups. Librarians and educators can link these together in a series to serve particular age groups. In addition, many of these programs are easily adapted to different age groups or family audiences with a range of ages. Consider linking them in program series around specific topics or themes like the following:

Video and Media Production: Time-Lapse Germination, Action Figure Party, Now in Theaters, Animated Name Video, Video Survey, and Two-Minute Memoir.

Photo Production and Image Editing: Lego Self-Portrait, Illustrated Acrostic, Photo 101, Comic Instructions, Design Workshop, Logo Maker.

STEM (Science, Technology, Engineering and Mathematics) Focus: Climate, Graphing Pollution, The Moon, Introduction to the Solar System, Time-Lapse Germination, App Concept Design, Headline Discussion (focused on science news).

Figure 1.1.
Children at work during an iPad program. Planning with crayons and a storyboard helps focus their efforts on the device.

Photo by Joel A. Nichols

From *iPads in the Library: Using Tablet Technology to Enhance Programs for All Ages* by Joel A. Nichols.
Santa Barbara, CA: Libraries Unlimited. Copyright © 2013.

Workforce Development Programs: Resumes, Interview Prep, Effective Presentations, App Concept Design, Two-Minute Memoir, and Trolley, Train or Rail, English Conversation Practice.

Small Business and Entrepreneurship: Effective Presentations, Logos, App Concept Design, Local Resources for New Americans (adapted for business resources), Interview Preparation Workshop, Photo 101, Now in Theaters (to create a trailer for a business, for example).

Engaging Seniors: eReader Program, Adaptive Tools, Brain Games, Virtual Museum Visits, Visual Recipe Potluck, Headline Discussion, Trolley, Train or Rail, Two-Minute Memoir.

Plan and schedule a programming series to help build an audience. Consider structuring these programs as part of regularly scheduled iPad labs in attractive time slots: afterschool science, midmorning preschool or senior events, evening or weekend family events, and so on. Cycle through and conduct these programs with the same audiences more than once, and you will find that your audiences come up with something newer, funnier and more creative every time.

NOTE

1. Ian Paul, "Apple CEO Cook Says iPad Tablets Will Outsell PCs," *PC World*, February 18, 2012, http://www.pcworld.com/article/250008/apple_ceo_cook_says_ipad_tablets_will_outsell_pcs.html (accessed October 14, 2012).

1

Device Management Best Practices

IPADS AND IOS

The first iPad was released in 2010. It did not have a camera, and the iOS did not support much interactivity between apps. The programs and apps in this book were tested on iPad 2s running version 6 of iOS. The next iPad to be introduced, called simply the iPad, featured improved resolution and display. In addition, a third iPad model (simply called "iPad") and an iPad Mini that is smaller in size have come out. There are also several models of iPod touch on which many of these programs (and apps) will work. Be sure to check primarily for operating system version and whether or not there are the necessary cameras you need for any particular program.

In this vein, most of these programs will also work well on other tablet platforms. Search other app stores for equivalent versions of the apps. Some of the apps used in this book have Android versions, and in many cases there are completely different Android apps with similar content and function.

IPAD TIPS AND BEST PRACTICES

1. Use iTunes to manage the devices. Install iTunes on your desktop or laptop, and then you can download apps and transfer them to the iPad via USB. This also makes it easier to "image" the iPads, or to make sure that the same apps are loaded on all of them.
2. Use one iTunes account to manage your iPads. Pay for an app once and use it on all your devices. The user licenses for apps allow for this kind of use with multiple devices and one iTunes account. Create a new, unique Gmail account for this iTunes account, so you can share it with other staff easily (for example, LibraryiPads@gmail.com). Download an app once and use it on multiple devices at once. Create this iTunes account on a computer rather than on the iPad. When you create iTunes accounts on a computer, you are not required to enter a credit card number to create the account. On an iPad, the credit card is required.

Donna — did you know this !

3. If you are going to buy apps, buy an iTunes gift card rather than tie a personal credit card to this account. This will keep your personal data private.

4. Familiarize yourself with the settings app. Unlike desktop operating systems, where you can find something like a "file" or "settings" menu inside a particular software application, iOS apps often do not have settings that are manageable from inside themselves. Instead, you will see settings options for any particular app inside the main settings application.

5. Create a numbered naming convention for your iPads (e.g., StorytimeiPad1, StorytimeiPad2, etc.). This will help you keep track of which is which when they are synching, and it will help if you decide to let patrons use them in house. Find this menu:

   Settings → General → About → Name

6. Make sure your iPad has the most current version of iOS running. (That should be iOS 6 as of January 2013). To check, go here:

   Settings → General → About → Software Update

7. Store the log-on credentials—Wi-Fi signal name or password—so the iPads connect automatically. Troubleshoot your connectivity here:

   Settings → Wi-Fi

8. Use security settings to disable the app store, and to disable the ability to delete or download apps during programs:

   Settings → General → About → Restrictions

9. Avoid putting your own personal accounts on these apps: Mail, Facebook, Twitter, and so on. If you are using the apps when traveling to a conference, then it makes sense. If not, particularly if the iPads will be used by the public, this is a security and privacy risk.

10. Take screenshots by holding down both buttons. Not all apps come with the functionality to preserve the project you are working on, or to take screenshots. iPads have a built-in screenshot tool that works anywhere on the device and with any programs. Simply press down the home button and the sleep button at the same time. A screenshot will automatically save to your Photo Roll.

11. Use **Dropbox** and/or email accounts. Moving files on and off the iPad can be difficult in library settings because you do not want your personal email or users' email accounts on the devices. Webmail applications can be unpredictable via Safari, as well, especially with attachments. To avoid these problems, use **Dropbox**, a file-sharing app. Install it on any computer and download the app on the iPad. You can drag or save any file from your PC into the Dropbox folder, which is also then available via the **Dropbox** app on the iPad. Remember that some file formats will not work. Similarly, you can create generic email addresses for your devices, if desired, so that you and users can email files to and from the iPad.

2

App Selection Criteria

Just as with selection of any other library materials, professional reviews are invaluable to selecting apps. See below for recommended app review resources. Do keep in mind, though, that there are many reasons why quality apps may have no reviews.

First, with hundreds of thousands of apps, it is easy to get lost in the crowd. Second, apps themselves are relatively new. Tablet devices are within the first five years of their lives, as are the app stores and apps that provide their software. The practice of reviewing them in professional literature is therefore in its infancy. Third, Apple promotes some apps by sending them to the top of category lists. These apps are more likely to be reviewed or promoted on parenting blogs, educational technology blogs, and websites. However, these apps are probably backed by larger marketing budgets. For these reasons, app selectors sometimes have to do more digging. This involves more than looking for the app equivalents of things that collection development librarians know to be wary of in books: vanity publishers and political ideologies, flashy covers that hide shallow information, or, worse, inaccurate information. Very small-scale developers can sign up with the iTunes, write an excellent app, and then sell it through the store. But they are sometimes less likely to be reviewed.

All apps for the iPad have to be purchased and downloaded in the iTunes Store. Android apps come from the Google store, Google Play; some Android-based tablets such as the Kindle Fire or the Nook also have their own app stores on Amazon or Barnes and Noble, respectively. The iTunes store is an online markpetplace also sell music, television shows and movies, books, and more. There is no alternative place to buy apps, and users should remember that the goal of the iTunes App Store is to sell you apps and for you to spend money on them. Therefore, you cannot trust reviews or categories blindly, and you need to be on the lookout for scam apps that come with no real function or content.

Another challenge in purchasing apps is that the iTunes store is browsable only by using iTunes and not via a web browser. The iTunes store does maintain a mirror

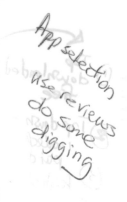

website that duplicates all of the app records in the store on webpages. However, it does not duplicate the categories or navigation of the iTunes store.

For librarians used to selecting books with several browser windows open—such as a vendor database to select titles, Global Books in Print to verify information, the library's OPAC for reference, and even sites such as GoogleBooks or Amazon.com to read reviews to see inside the book to switch between—the App Store is lesson after lesson in inconvenience because one can look at only one app record at a time.

One can browse and search the store from the iPad itself, or from a desktop or laptop computer with iTunes. Because iTunes does not browse like a webpage (no tabs or multiple windows), the store is particularly clunky when accessed from the iPad itself. It is difficult to keep track of where you have browsed and what you have researched already and what you have not; there is also a noticeable time lag after tapping on an app's record before the pages with more complete information load. Therefore, I recommend selecting apps from a desktop or laptop via iTunes. Wired Internet connections will likely be faster than wireless ones, so downloading apps and then transferring them via USB cable to the iPad will be quicker. Or, if multiple devices are synched with the same iTunes ID and set to download apps automatically, the iPads will start downloading and updated themselves as you do it on the desktop or laptop.

ITUNES STORE TIPS

Keep in mind that iPhone apps will also run on the iPad, albeit at a lower resolution or smaller size. Click "iPad" at the top of the app store to see only iPad apps. Use the categories. From Books and Business to Education, Health and Fitness and Lifestyle to Entertainment, Medical and Travel to Photo and Video Production, and so on, this is the most powerful way Apple offers to sort the apps based on subject.

On the front page of the store, you will find listings of the top-selling apps in three categories: the top downloaded free apps, the top downloaded pay apps, and the highest grossing apps. The first 10 in each are listed, and then there is a link to see the entire top 200. This feature is useful because it shows what apps other users are buying and downloading. These apps will tend to have more reviews, and it will be easier to find online tutorials or other information about them in support forums.

You can also use the search box to find apps. App and company names are searchable, as well as some keywords. Run a few sample searches and then start clicking to experience some of the inconveniences previously mentioned. After looking at an app in detail, returning to the search results brings users back to the beginning of the search results, even if the results page you had just clicked from was several pages down. In addition, even if you attempt to set search limits for iPad apps only, the store will likely refresh those criteria and also offer you music, movies, or books. In response, there are third-party apps whose purpose is searching the App Store. Yes, you can download an app whose primary function is searching for other apps in the App Store. Two (of the many) to try out are **Chomp** and **App Shopper**. These apps will also help you find apps on sale.

Also, the good news is that most of the apps are fairly cheap, usually $0.99 or $1.99. Of course, some are dramatically more costly. The iOS analogues to the Microsoft Office suite (**Pages**, **Numbers**, and **Keynote**) cost $9.99 each, for example, and many of the free or cheaper alternatives do not come close to these apps in terms of functionality.

The store contains a brief summary of the app written by the developers, and screenshots of the app in use. Be wary of any apps that do not show screenshots. Examine these closely. Does the content match up with the description? Can you see menu and navigation options on the screenshots that seem to match the description in the store? If something seems inconsistent with the screenshots, search online for a tutorial or video of someone using that app. If you cannot find any, it might mean the app is not worth your purchase.

Also use the customer reviews. Sometimes, when there are few, their usefulness is limited, and keep in mind that Apple reserves the right to delete or modify any review. One helpful tip is to sort the reviews by "Most Critical" instead of the default sort option, which is "Most Positive."

ESSENTIAL APP REVIEW SOURCES

The APPitic (http://adeapps.com), a cooperative of teachers (Apple's Distinguished Educators) that curates best-of apps lists for educational settings. This site boasts over 1,800 apps for education. These apps are browsable in categories: New, SPED and Autism, Preschool, Themes, Multiple Intelligences, Bloom's Taxonomy, and others. Each features pricing information and a short phrase summing up the app. Click on the app for a longer review and for many screenshots.

Boing Boing's Apps for Kids (http://boingboing.net/tag/appsforkids) is a collaborative effort between writer and editor Mark Frauenfelder and his daughter Jane. It offers kid-centric and parent-approved reviews of smartphone apps for kids across various platforms, so not all the apps reviewed are available for the iPad.

iPad Insight (http://ipadinsight.com) is a blog about all things iPad. While it certainly has a commercial bent (lots of new cases to buy and promotional posts), it also contains useful app reviews and timely news about changes in software or hardware. Each week they post a Best Free iPad App of the Week, which sometimes is a powerful pay app on promotional sale or free. Navigate the top navigation links to read a list of the Best Free Apps, iPad App Reviews, and iPad Tips & Tricks.

School Library Journal (http://www.slj.com/category/books-media/reviews/digital-resources) now reviews apps along with other digital resources. This excellent professional resource is a great place to read about new apps of interest to librarians and teachers, and to read professional reviews you can rely on.

TCEA (Texas Computer Education Association; http://www.tcea.org/ipad) is an organized devoted to integrating technology into the classroom. This list of iPad apps is sorted by subject area: language arts, math, science, social studies, interactive books, primary grades, other subjects, special needs, and tools, and it even has a listing of websites to use via the Safari app that are educationally powerful. Inside each category, apps are organized by more specific topic; for example, in the math category, there are columns for apps that support counting/number lines, addition, subtraction, multiplication, division, money, word problems, decimals, algebra, geometry, reading and creating graphs, and so on. One of the best features of this site is that it lists these similar apps side by side, making it easy to find a free substitute for a pay app with similar functionality.

Touch and Go (http://blog.schoollibraryjournal.com/touchandgo), a *School Library Journal* blog edited by Daryl Grabarek, reviews the best apps for children and teens. New posts are published three times a week, and all reviews are archived in *School Library Journal*'s Database.

3

Programs for Children Aged Birth to Five

USING SCREENS WITH VERY YOUNG CHILDREN: RELUCTANT TECHNOLOGY FOR THE UNDER FIVES

iPads are highly popular and thrillingly attractive to young children. I see it in the library, of course, when conducting iPad programs with children. I also see it when a parent hands an iPhone to a toddler when waiting in a long checkout line, kids using iPads or other tablets to play games or consume media in airports or on my trolley ride every day, and among my friends and family, some of whom have very "wired" kids who easily play **Angry Birds** or **Temple Run**, always demand to see the picture of themselves just taken on a smartphone, or helpfully know to return to the main screen on an app when their adult is at a loss.

But are any of these activities good for them? Below you will find fun and engaging programs for very young children that are based in the important preliteracy skills children need in order to become successful readers. Ultimately, however, time on a tablet or a smartphone is still screen time. The latest recommendations from the ADAM Medical Encyclopedia from the National Library of Medicine/National Institutes of Health, accessed via Medline, are quite strict. The encyclopedia recommends no screen time at all for anyone under two years old, and limiting it to just one to two hours a day for children over two, reminding parents that there is no evidence that "educational" video or multimedia content is in fact beneficial to developing children.[1] Consider conveying information about these limits at your programs so parents are making informed choices.

A crucial difference with these programs is a larger degree of interactivity than your average cartoon episode. First of all, parents need active roles in these programs; and secondly, none of these programs or apps is designed for children to passively observe or consume the media. Instead, they are tracing letter shapes and practicing sounds, making a game out of a photograph with their parent or caregiver, and so on. These need to be active and interactive programs, with a skilled adult (librarian or teacher) interacting with the program participants, prompting children to discover these content and skills; and the programs should include nondigital components whenever possible to make it relevant to users who do not have access to these tools at home.

BABY & ME APP EXPLORATION

Goal: Parents and babies explore early literacy apps together in a one-on-one setting, and then to share with other parents what worked and what they liked.

Apps: Letters A to Z, Literacy Skills Sampler HD, Singing Fingers, Letter Tracer

Planning Notes: Give participants plenty of time to explore the apps they are interested in, to ask questions, and to get feedback from the other participants. End the program by bringing everyone back together for a closing song or fingerplay, and ask if anyone has any other early literacy apps they recommend. Be sure to pass out an evaluation card so participants can comment specifically on each app. Their feedback about which apps they liked and which they would use again in the library or at home will improve the next Baby & Me App Exploration program.

Books/Other Materials: *Goodnight, iPad* by Ann Droyd, a technoparody of Margaret Wise Brown's *Goodnight, Moon* that is appropriate for all ages.

Instructions:
Treat this program like a baby storytime, and start with at least one song or fingerplay. If delivering the song or fingerplay via iPad, consider:

- Using a special song from the collection; use a desktop or laptop computer to import this song into iTunes, and then transfer the songs to the iPad to play in the program.
- Accompanying yourself with a video fingerplay from King County's Wiki (http://wiki.kcls.org/tellmeastory/index.php/Main_Page)
- Making a felt animation with **Felt Board** and **SlideShare** (see the following Baby Storytime program for instructions about sharing a **Felt Board** story via **SlideShare**).

First, demonstrate each app for the parents.

Letters A to Z

Open this app to reveal every letter of the alphabet on colored blocks. Select a letter and the block enlarges and takes the center part of the screen. Each letter has an accompanying illustration (A is for apple, K is koala, etc.).

Demonstrate this app by reciting the ABC song and tapping each letter as you say it. Suggest that parents start not with A, but rather with the first letter of their child's name, or with M for mom/mama or P or D for papa/dad.

With older toddlers who are already on their way to knowing the alphabet song, challenge parents to start with Z and say the alphabet backwards. This pattern disruption can isolate letters children might be having trouble with, and can also reinvigorate parents and children bored with the same old storytime songs.

Tap the "I" icon in the lower right-hand corner to enable the limited options in this program. This displays lowercase letters on the blocks, which is another great way to enhance letter knowledge. The other option will play the phoneme associated with the letter, which is a way of incorporating phonological awareness and the sounds letters make into the program.

Figure 3.1

Letters A to Z. Move easily among the letter shapes and sounds by scrolling up and down in the left hand navigation ribbon.

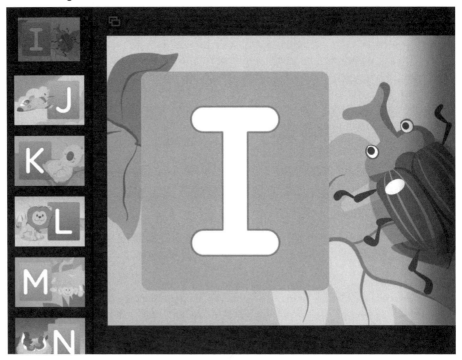

Screenshot courtesy True-Learning.

Singing Fingers

This finger-painting app also records any sounds while you finger paint; and the app is simple enough for toddlers to use on their own.

Multicolored dots appear anywhere you tap or drag your fingertips. While you are drawing, try singing an appropriate song or reciting a chant or fingerplay. For example, doodle star shapes while singing "Twinkle, Twinkle, Little Star," or name the names of objects: draw a circle and say "circle," or "ball." When participants are done finger painting, they can press anywhere on their drawing and listen to what they just recorded.

These finger paintings with sound might be the first electronic media ever produced by these eventual digital natives!

The main controls are icons in the upper left of the screen. Participants can clear the screen by tapping on the new blank document icon (looks like a piece of paper), save their work with the disk icon, and access saved pages by tapping on the folder icon.

You can take a screenshot of the children's creation to print out or email as a take-away from this program. (Unfortunately, there is no way to export the recorded media with the drawing, so users will not have a record of their voices in their creation.)

Letter Tracer

This app is perfect for children who are starting to write and recognize their letters. The concept is simple: participants trace letter or number shapes in order to practice these letter shapes.

Note that this app is optimized for the iPhone, so although you can use it magnified with resolution loss, it is best to stick with the smaller screen area because that is a better size for children's fingers and hands.

Tap the pen icon along the bottom navigation ribbon to change the display from black block letters to letters outlined in black but with white space inside the outline. In the white space mode, children can trace the shape. Their fingers will make a colored line (the default is red) wherever they trace, tap, or touch.

Tap the settings icon. The top row of options allows you to adjust between uppercase and lowercase letters, as well as to pick numbers.

The second row of icons offers two modes for tracing. In the first, participants trace the letter shape inside the black lines. In the second, participants are given a smaller letter as a model and must write the letter without the guidelines. The third row of options is for setting the voice output—none, female, male, or child. The fourth row is a slider bar to select volume levels for the voice output. The last two rows are a slider bar to select pen thickness—thicker lines tend to work a little better for younger children—and to adjust the color of the pen from the default red to any other color available. Tap "Done" to save these settings and to return to the tracing board.

Trace away! Advance to the next letter by pressing the left or right arrows on the bottom navigation row. They will advance in alphabetical order. To sort the letters randomly—again, as a way to increase the challenge level for participants already comfortable with many letters—click the shuffle icon shaped like two intersecting arrows

Literacy Skills Sampler HD

Although this app is designed to support adult learners, it could also be useful for parents and children to explore together. While some of the words it shows are common sight words for kindergartners, such as "eyes" or "pen" or "run," there are also more difficult and conceptual words such as "think," "thank," "week," and "wallet." This app supports functional literacy and matches each word with a series of photos or videos that illustrate that work.

Tap "eye," and a short slideshow starts. It shows the word EYE on the first slide; then several photographs of people's eyes, of people with animals, etc.; and then ends with the word EYE again on the last slide.

Challenge participants in your group to pick one or two words to learn together from this sampler list.

FACE GAME

Goal: Parents or caregivers make a game on the iPad using a photograph of themselves or their child, and then play that game with their toddler.

Apps: TinyTap, Camera

Planning Notes: Nestle this game-making program in a short-story program using an excellent toddler or easy picture book about the body parts, facial features, or clothing.

Books/Other Materials: *Ella Sarah Gets Dressed* by Margaret Chodos Irvine.

Instructions:
TinyTap works by using verbal prompts—i.e., "point to baby's chin"—tied to specific areas defined on a photograph. If the child taps the defined areas, a balloon shows success. If not, an animated cloud drifts away from the area to show they have tapped the wrong area.

Games are made up of pages, and you can create a multiple-step game by using additional pages.

1. Introduce the app by showing a sample game. You can even make a one-page game in front of everyone while they watch if you have presentation equipment.
2. Demonstrate how to use the camera. Be sure to let participants know what will happen to the pictures after the program (erasing is best practice), and also let them know that you will also erase the game they make after the program. The games on this app are not exportable, so one way for participants to have a take-home, if desired, would be to take a screen shot of their game and offer to email or print it.
3. Games have two options: (1) an overarching question, where the participant answers the same question on multiple pages (see sample included with app "Who Is Bigger"); or (2) one image with several different questions. The Face Game is one of the latter. This app comes with a sample game, and also has a "store" link that brings you to other games for free and for purchase.
4. Be sure to show your participants both the front facing and the back facing cameras, and demonstrate the difference in video size shooting with the iPad in landscape versus portrait mode. As with most photo options in apps, you can either import a photo from the **Photo Roll** or take one inside the app.
5. Open the app and have everyone take/import a photo of their face or their child's face. Anyone concerned with privacy should be encouraged to use an object instead, and you should have puppets, stuffed animals, or action figures on hand.
6. Add questions, for which you can also record a message that plays for the correct answer as well as for incorrect ones. Once the question is recorded, follow the on-screen prompts and trace the area of the photograph with your fingertip that corresponds to the prompt. A dotted line will mark the area you have identified.
7. Remind participants that they can edit, rerecord, and retrace the targets on their game pages as many times as they want.

When the games are finished, let the children play them. If participants are willing, families can trade devices and play each other's games.

From *iPads in the Library: Using Tablet Technology to Enhance Programs for All Ages* by Joel A. Nichols. Santa Barbara, CA: Libraries Unlimited. Copyright © 2013.

Figure 3.2

One of **TinyTap**'s built-in games: tap the mouse that is hiding behind the piece of cheese.

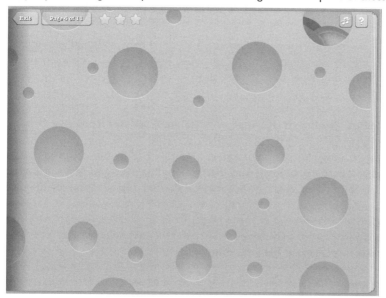

Screenshot courtesy TinyTap.

Figure 3.3

If you find the mouse, your success is marked by a balloon.

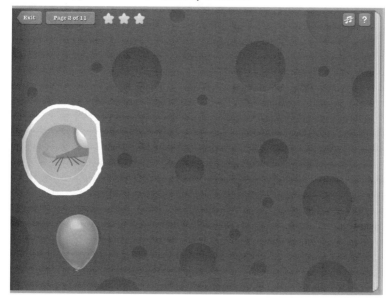

Screenshot courtesy TinyTap.

BABY STORYTIME

Goal: Deliver songs, noises, and picture books in a baby and toddler storytime on the iPad. Great baby storytimes are short, engaging programs that offer a few songs, fingerplays, or books as well as time for parents to socialize and make connections while their babies play.

Apps: Safari, FeltBoard, Keynote or SlideShark, eBook Reader of choice

Planning Notes: This program is ideal for birth to 18 months, although as with most baby storytimes, older brothers and sisters should be welcome. Have everyone sit in a semicircle on the floor. Begin with a song. If desired, play the song on the iPad.

Books/Other Materials: Favorite books for baby storytime, such as titles by Tana Hoban, Donald Crews, or Simms Taback; other board books for playtime; appropriate toys, shaker eggs, etc. for baby playtime.

Instructions:
Do a fingerplay. See the King County Library System Tell Me a Story Wiki at http://tiny.cc/kccw for many examples. If desired, show parents this resource at the end of the program for them to use at home.

1. Present a digital felt story. Use the **FeltBoard** app. Prepare the background you want ahead of time and have the figures out of the dock for easy access by tapping any figure in the navigation ribbon to appear on your background.
2. In descending order, the icons show the available characters and patterns. They are: people and human shapes, clothing, pets, nature shapes, letters, and numbers. Move the shapes into desired position. Pinch to make them bigger or smaller.
3. As you advance your story, drag any shapes or figures you are done with to the trash. This technique works well with reductive stories or songs such as "Five Green and Speckled Frogs."
4. In case this live **FeltBoard** is not your style, consider still using the felt board to prepare a slideshow you can use to tell your story, Kamishibai-style. Kamishibai refers to a Japanese storytelling technique based on heavily illustrated cards. The storyteller tells the story by describing the first card in the deck, and then pulls it around
5. To make something like "Five Green and Speckled Frogs" in this style, chose the pond background from the template. Then select the Animals icon, and pull out five frogs from the icon drawer. Also put out the numbers 1, 2, 3, 4, and 5. Be sure to push the icon drawer back in by tapping the brown arrow.
6. Enlarge the frogs and the numbers. If you have a way to project the iPad screen onto the wall or to mirror it on a larger display, do so. If not, be prepared to pass it in front of everyone's eyes.
7. Arrange the numbers in descending order along the edge of the pond. Then, drag the frogs on top of them to obscure them. There will be no number behind one of the frogs (unless you are

From *iPads in the Library: Using Tablet Technology to Enhance Programs for All Ages* by Joel A. Nichols. Santa Barbara, CA: Libraries Unlimited. Copyright © 2013.

trying to incorporate zero), and the numeral 5 will be out on its own and not hiding behind a frog.

8. Now take a screenshot by tapping the camera icon on the right. Then drag the numeral 5 to the trash, and the frog in front of the numeral 4. Take a screenshot. Repeat this action until you have a screenshot showing each number of frogs. Also, take a screenshot of the blank pond landscape to match up with the last line, "and then there were no more green and speckled frogs."

9. Next, make a slideshow of these images using **Keynote**. Open **Keynote**, click the plus sign to create a new project, and then import the photos you want and arrange them on slides. You could also use any other slideshow application (or PowerPoint on a PC) to create this slideshow and then view and play it back on the iPad using **SlideShark**.

10. Email the PowerPoint presentation to the iPad. Tap and hold on the attachment, and a menu will pop up offering you the option to "Open in SlideShark."

11. Offer another picture or board book. Consider, if you want, using the eReader of your choice to deliver the story.

End with another fingerplay or closing song. Make iPads available during playtime, if desired, for parents to experiment with the apps or for older toddlers to play with the **FeltBoard** app. Remember that play is better for baby brain development than screen-time, so limit the iPad exploration accordingly.

Figure 3.4
FeltBoard's interactive play space allows you and your audiences to customize and resize characters, backgrounds and objects.

Screenshot courtesy FeltBoard.

T IS FOR TODDLER

Goal: Toddlers and their caregivers practice two key early literacy skills, letter knowledge and phonological awareness, in an interactive story and game environment.

Apps: Monsters Socks, Letter Tracer, TinyTap, ePicture Books about the alphabet (such as *Chicka Chicka Boom Boom* by Bill Martin Jr. or *LMNOPeas* by Keith Baker) or whatever is available.

Planning Notes: Use **TinyTap**'s built-in games or download free ones from the in-app store for this program. In advance of the program, make a game in **TinyTap** that pairs letter sounds that you record with letters. This program is a perfect opportunity to educate parents about hands-on early literacy practices. Letter knowledge is an important preliteracy skill, and it means that children know the names of the letters and are familiar with their shape. The more familiar children are with the letters and what they look like, the more native and comfortable reading becomes.[2] The other preliteracy skill this program practices is phonological knowledge, which has to do with sounds and the sounds that make up words.

Books/Other Materials: *It Looked Like Spilt Milk* by Charles G. Shaw; *Dinosaur Roar* by Paul and Henrietta Strickland; *LMNOPeas* by Keith Baker; and *Chicka, Chicka, Boom, Boom* by Bill Martin Jr.

Instructions:
Sing, read, or felt board your favorite alphabet book or alphabet song. Consider delivering it via iPad, if applicable.

Go around the circle and ask everyone to say what their favorite letter or the letter that begins their first name. Be sure to include your name or L for Library in the circle.

1. Hand out the iPads and open **Letter Tracer**. Use **Letter Tracer** so participants can practice tracing the outline of a letter or number with their fingers, practicing writing the letter shape.
2. Tap the pen icon along the bottom navigation ribbon to change the display from black-block letters to letters outlined in black but with white space inside the outline.
3. Tap the settings icon. The top row of options allows you to adjust between uppercase and lowercase letters, as well as to pick numbers. Stick with uppercase in this program.
4. Use the slider bar on the second-to-last row to select pen the thickest pen size available and change the ink color if you want. Tap "Done" to save these settings and to return to the tracing board.
5. Advance to the next letter by pressing the left or right arrows on the bottom navigation row. The letters will advance in alphabetical order.
6. Ask toddlers to call out the name of the letter they are tracing, or challenge them and their parents to find their special letter and just do that one. Collect the iPads.

Sing an active song that ends with everyone well settled at the end, such as "Five Green and Speckled Frogs" or another circle time favorite. Read another picture book,

From *iPads in the Library: Using Tablet Technology to Enhance Programs for All Ages* by Joel A. Nichols. Santa Barbara, CA: Libraries Unlimited. Copyright © 2013.

either explicitly about letters or one that extends the theme, such as *LMNOPeas* by Keith Baker or *Chicka, Chicka, Boom, Boom* by Bill Martin Jr. Remember to integrate letter-knowledge and phonological awareness into your reading, especially if you have chosen something other than an alphabet book. Frame the story with the following questions and challenges:

We are on a hunt for letters. When you see or hear the letter your name begins with, snap your fingers (or wave your fingers or whatever easy gesture will not be too disruptive to your group). The parents will mostly be the ones recognizing letters and helping the gesture, so nearly anything works.

Does anyone's name in here begin with the same letter as "dinosaur"?

Hand out the iPads and play the **TinyTap** game. Remember that you will either preselect one of the **TinyTap** games that come with the app or download a free one from their marketplace. Baby Dino and Cloud Gazing are two free ones to try, and they can tie in with the optional picture books suggested above.

Offer felt or paper letters if there are not enough iPads to go around. After five minutes or so of playing **TinyTap**, bring everyone together for a closing song or story of your choices.

Figure 3.5
Toy Blocks's three-dimension build space lets kids rotate their creations and add on from any direction.

Screenshot courtesy Toy Blocks/SIXCLICK Inc.

ASSEMBLY REQUIRED

Goal: To expose preschoolers to simple shape and building concepts.

Apps: Lego 4+ (note that it only works in landscape), **Toy Blocks**, **K-Magic**

Books/Other Materials: *Castle* by David MacCauley (or other similar title); *Not a Box* by Antoinette Portis; physical building blocks or Legos.

Instructions:

Use **K-Magic**'s movie option to play a short animated story about friends helping each other out. They move blocks together and stand on each other's shoulders to reach higher. It helps set the tone for this program, both with the blocks and in terms of cooperation if the participants are sharing devices.

1. Open **Toy Blocks**. Demonstrate how to place blocks on the three-dimensional grid. First, tap the single green block. A menu pops up where you can select block size/style, and also shape. Select the style and shape you want, and then tap again on the grid. Tap anywhere on the grid and a block will appear. Tap it again to make it go away. Begin building the desired shape by placing blocks next to each other and on top of each other.
2. Be sure to leave **Lego 4+** until last, or children will not use the other two apps. This is really a simple video game with familiar Lego characters, but at the beginning of each level, users have to assemble the vehicle and other Lego shapes.
3. The app is very intuitive, and animated arrows show users where and how to swipe their fingers to advance the action. The game play is a slow and simple driving game across a gently rolling landscape where users attempt to collect coins.
4. Special interstitial levels bring users into another game space, a three-dimensional arena, where they must assemble a Lego shape. These levels are more difficult because the Lego shapes are more like puzzles. It is still intuitive enough for most four- and five-year-olds.
5. Use any physical blocks or other manipulatives to supplement how many tablet devices you have, and also to give the children the experience of building in both digital and physical media. Have the books about buildings and structures on display, and encourage the audience to explore them at the end of the program.

Take and print or email screenshots of the structures completed, so children will have something to take home from this program.

NOTES

1. http://www.nlm.nih.gov/medlineplus/ency/patientinstructions/000355.htm
2. *Every Child Ready to Read*, Second Edition Kit. Published by ALSC & PLA, 2011.

From *iPads in the Library: Using Tablet Technology to Enhance Programs for All Ages* by Joel A. Nichols. Santa Barbara, CA: Libraries Unlimited. Copyright © 2013.

4

Programs for School-Aged Children

FAMILY BILINGUAL STORYTIME

Goals: For librarians who know only English to learn to present a bilingual story program for a family crowd, and also to recruit parent volunteers who could help with the next bilingual program you could do.

Apps: iTranslate, iTunes, YouTube content via Safari, Maps, Felt Board

Books/Other Materials: Picture books in English and in the target language; songs in the target language; books about animal noises work especially well, such as *Animals Speak* by Lila Prap; physical felt board and patterns.

Instructions:
To use **iTranslate**, use the settings option (gear icon) in the upper left of the screen. There you can select your source and target languages, as well as other usability options, including a dictionary option, detecting end of speech, auto speech, and shake to speech. It works well with these options set to "on."

1. Shake the device, and the flag icon on the left will illuminate. Speak into the microphone and watch as the app dictates what you have written and translates it into the target language on the other side of the screen. Hold the microphone close to your mouth and speak clearly.
2. Tap the speaker icon at the bottom of the screen in the middle to adjust the voice quality for each language. You can pick a masculine- or feminine-sounding voice and adjust the rate at which the app speaks.
3. If there are errors, especially because of background noise, you can correct them by tapping on the text you want to edit. The keyboard will pop up for you to type in your phrase.

From *iPads in the Library: Using Tablet Technology to Enhance Programs for All Ages* by Joel A. Nichols. Santa Barbara, CA: Libraries Unlimited. Copyright © 2013.

It works best to pass the device back and forth, especially if you have to rely on the keyboard options. Unfortunately, languages written in alphabets other than the Latin one are not represented by appropriate keyboard support.

This program delivers a bilingual story program and suggests ways an iPad can help even monolingual librarians offer an engaging, multicultural, and/or multilingual program for children of all ages and their caregivers.

Use this app fairly judiciously. Although functional, it will not offer a nonspeaker the finesse and polish you want for extremely formal presentations.

Use it to welcome the crowd to the library and to introduce yourself. Then encourage everyone else to introduce themselves and their family, using whatever language they would like. Feel free to pass the device around for people who want to translate their own introduction for fellow participants.

Plan a story program with a few picture books, songs, or movement rhymes. Use your library collection or the iTunes Store to find songs or rhymes in the target language or bilingual songs. There are many options for simple songs. If you are having trouble, focus on (1) numbers, (2) colors, or (3) simple animal songs. Colors and numbers are a great beginning to learning words in a new language, and having a limited subset makes it easier to remember the new vocabulary. If possible, pick songs that you know in English. There are readily available versions in Spanish and Chinese and many other languages of "Head, Shoulders, Knees and Toes," the "Itsy-Bitsy Spider," and so on. Print out the lyrics in the target language to have on hand to help yourself and to help participants.

Use **YouTube** or **Safari** to play any foreign language song or fingerplay for the audience. Or, if you are using CDs from the Library collection, rip the music into iTunes, and then transfer the songs to the iPad using a cable or via the cloud.

1. Read or tell the first story in English. Do not attempt to translate it with the app. But do use iTranslate to introduce the book, by saying something like, "Now we're going to read about the little red hen that ends up doing all the hard work!"
2. Then play one of the songs in the target language that you have located. Follow that by singing the song in English. Be sure to hand out bilingual lyrics for everyone. Remember that everyone will be differently bilingual and have different levels of literacy in the languages they speak at home and in English.

Feel free to keep repeating these songs until everyone has time to stretch their brain to accommodate new words, new lyrics, new rhythms, and new languages.

Use the **FeltBoard** app or an actual felt board to tell a story in English. Now prompt the participants to help you tell the story again in the target language. This could be as elaborate as a totally translated story, or as simple as substitution of vocabulary words. For example, if you are using the "Three Little Pigs," perhaps the wolf knocks on the "puerta" instead of the door, or in the second, bilingual retelling of the "Little Red Hen," you tell the story in English but use the character names in another language (la gallinita roja, el cerdo, el gato, el pato, for example, in Spanish).

Be sure to read at least one book about animal noises, or about saying hello in different languages. If you have only an animal noises book in English, read it, but ask participants to make the sounds that animals make in their language, too. While you can use **iTranslate** to help facilitate these questions, most parents—even if they do not speak or understand English—will understand the task after seeing the book in English and hearing you and the crowd make the noises.

Consider ending with another bilingual song or a song twice, once in English and once in the target language, and making the **Maps** app available for people to show each other where they are from.

You could also have one large paper map on the wall or on a flannel board, and ask parents and children to point out where they and their families have connections.

Figure 4.1

Use **FeltBoard** to tell a story in English, and then invite the parents or teachers in the audience to help you retell it in the target language.

Screenshot Software Smoothie

CLASSROOM VISIT

Goal: Create an effective and dazzling classroom visit promoting library services and programs.

Apps: Camera, FeltBoard, Magic Stage App, Keynote or SlideShark, Brainquest, Safari

Planning Notes: Before you meet, prepare a photo slideshow of the library, starting with the front door and focusing largely on the children's areas and collection. Show off approximately 5–10 photos of programs, popular materials, or displays, the library computers or iPads, etc., to entice children to come to the library. Photos look great on the iPad display, but you will want to walk around the room so everyone can see a couple of the shots up close. Simply show these photos from the camera roll, or use **Keynote** or **SlideShark** to make a short slideshow presentation.

Books/Other Materials: High-interest picture books adaptable to many ages, such as *The Book That Eats People* by Mark Perry, *Go to Sleep, Gecko* by Margaret Read MacDonald, or *Chalk* by Bill Thompson.

Instructions:

Use **Brainquest** to play an interactive quiz game with the class. The free version of this app has timed rounds of seven questions on a variety of topics that are grouped by age group. Asking seven questions is plenty, and it will encourage kids to want to play more. This can be a great way to fill up time in case there is unexpected downtime or the visiting librarian needs more material. Questions range from Grades 1 through 5.

SlideShark is an app that enables viewing and sharing of PowerPoint and **Keynote** slideshows on the iPad. You cannot create a presentation in this app—you can only share one. But you can use a desktop computer and Microsoft PowerPoint to prepare your presentation ahead of time to deliver on the iPad. Upload the presentation to your free SlideShark account online from any computer, and then download it in the app. Open the app, log in, and then click the synch icon on the upper right of the screen. It looks like a circle made out of two arrows. (Note that you can also email PowerPoint presentations to the iPad. Tap and hold on the attachment, and a menu will pop up offering you the option to "Open in **SlideShark**.")

If you are using **Keynote**, you can create the presentation right on the iPad. Open **Keynote**, click the plus sign to create a new project, and then import the photos you want and arrange them on slides.

Perform at least one magic trick using the **Magic Stage App**. This app has three modes: clear, step-by-step tutorials with video and text, a video of someone else performing the trick, and then the trick mode itself. Use the tutorials and practice!

Two tricks that are easy to learn in five minutes or less each are the Thought Receiver and the Matchstick. In the first, participants name a color, and you input that color via secret and discreet taps. Then the participants put their fingertip on the screen and the viewer reveals which color they "named."

From *iPads in the Library: Using Tablet Technology to Enhance Programs for All Ages* by Joel A. Nichols. Santa Barbara, CA: Libraries Unlimited. Copyright © 2013.

Matchstick is a two-part trick. In the first, a similar set of secret tap inputs notes how many matchsticks are revealed in a box. Then, if you can palm a real matchstick successfully, you can tap the match on the screen. It disappears in a puff of digital smoke, and you can have a matchstick in your hand. Even if you cannot pull off the palming, children will still enjoy that the match disappears.

Read or tell a story to the class. Consider using an eBook or other electronic story format such as TumbleBooks, if your library subscribes to that resource, or use a printed book.

Ask students to help you recreate a scene from the story you just read using the **FeltBoard** app. Note that this will work best if you can project the iPad display onto screen or use a TV to mirror and enlarge the display. Open **FeltBoard**.

1. Tell students to pick a background, and tap on the uppermost icon (a blue-and-green square) on the left-hand navigation ribbon to display the predesigned felt backgrounds. There are backgrounds to suggest a forest, a movie theater, mountain landscapes, the surface of the moon, a pirate ship, or solid colors for a more abstract effect.
2. Tap the desired background template, and it will refresh in the main window. Then hide those options, tap again on the blue-and-green square icon, and the ribbon will slide back in to display the rest of the icons.
3. In descending order, the icons show the available characters and patterns. They are: people and human shapes, clothing, accessories (including magic wands and glasses!), pets, nature shapes, letters, and numbers.
4. Select the felt shapes you want to play with. Tap any figure in the navigation ribbon, and it will appear on your background in the main space.
5. Drag any unwanted shapes or figures into the trash. Anything selected appears on the felt-board space, so it is very easy to add shapes you did not mean to.
6. Move the shapes into desired position. Pinch to make them larger or smaller.
7. Tap the glue icon on the right side of the screen to affix certain shapes to the background, or to each other to make them easier to use. Tap the glue, then drag the drop of glue to the figure you intend to affix.

Use the camera icon to make a screenshot you can email back to the teacher to share with the class. This email is also a great opportunity to follow up on your class visit, and to publicize any library services you want.

FOLKTALES FOR SECOND GRADERS

Figure 4.2
A scuba diver and giant squid on the Moon are the tip of the iceberg among Toontastic's versatile scene and character options.

Screenshot courtesy Launchpad Toys

Goal: Remix a story with familiar and new fairy and folktale narratives, for a perfect activity for a class visit to the library or an after-school group.

App: Toontastic

Planning Notes: Toontastic's structure is better for longer cartoons and for younger audiences, but the only way to preserve or share these cartoons is via the Toontastic website, ToonTube. If you need or want to save the cartoon movie so you do not have share it online, use **PuppetPals HD** instead.

Books/Other Materials: Any fairy-tale favorite, from a simple Byron Barton version of *The Little Red Hen* or *The Three Bears*, or something such as John Scziescka's *The True Story of the Three Little Pigs*. For more advanced readers, consider reading up to three or four versions of the same story.

From *iPads in the Library: Using Tablet Technology to Enhance Programs for All Ages* by Joel A. Nichols. Santa Barbara, CA: Libraries Unlimited. Copyright © 2013.

Instructions:

In **Toontastic**, use the Parent Guide for further reference. Open Toontastic and tap "Create Cartoon." Tap "New Cartoon."

A Story Arc template comes with the app. Use the built-in story arc to help participants structure their cartoons. The standard arc here includes five scenes: Setup, Conflict, Challenge, Climax, and Resolution. If desired, walk participants through these terms. Or, challenge them to think about breaking up the fairy tale into five or fewer scenes.

1. To make the cartoon, select one of the scene blanks. Tap Setup, for example, and then tap the green paintbrush to edit that scene. Or, tap the red trash can to delete the scene.
2. Users can scroll through several predesigned settings, or import a photo of their own. For the purposes of this program, especially in a limited programming time, encourage them to use one of these backgrounds. Users will see a pirate ship, a castle scene, a lunar scene, and under-the-sea scene, and others. Encourage users to change the setting of the fairy tale in their retellings.
3. Select a setting, and then tap the white arrow pointing to the right. Next, participants can choose their Characters, or toys. Scroll to the left to show the available characters, and tap on them to select them. Tap the blinking arrow that points right. Resize the characters and setting by pinching and pulling, and then tap the green "Start Animation" button. Move the characters around with your fingers and speak their voices into the microphone. Once you have recorded the action, tap the red "Stop Animation" button. Whatever you have just animated will play back.
4. To move to the next scene, tap the blinking arrow in the upper right again, and add music. Choose based on emotional categories: friendly, happy, surprised, frustrated, sad, or nervous. Then edit each scene in the same way.
5. When users are done with their cartoon, tap "Done." Direct users to give it a title and list themselves as Director. Tap the check mark, and the movie will play. If desired, users can select the option to save on Toontastic's website, ToonTube, which requires creating an account. This is the only way to share or save videos from this app.

AFTER SCHOOL RESEARCH ORIENTATION

Goal: To teach reference skills to school-aged children. These can be used to demonstrate and explore your library website, electronic resources, and model effective Internet research skills. This works as a general overview and can be tailored to a specific set of topics and adapted to use during a class visit as well.

Apps: Safari, Merriam Webster HD, 3D CellStain, UN Country Stats, Science Glossary, Qwiki

Books/Other Materials: Be ready to point out reference books in the collection that provide comparison to these apps, and maybe have some high-interest reference books (DK series titles, titles about dinosaurs or skeletons, etc.) on display.

Instructions:

First, use **Safari** to explore the library website and catalog. Give participants practice searches to perform in the library catalog and in the library's electronic resources. For example, what books are available about the Harlem Renaissance? What short reference articles are available via databases? Are there any images or video available? Try any search terms appropriate to parts of the collection you would like to highlight or to the specified subjects.

Qwiki is a reference app with limited scope but a very engaging, photo-heavy interface for ready reference. The following categories are accessible on the interface: News, Local information, Popular, Actors, Cities, Natural Wonders, and Monuments. But the app has many more topics. While there are thousands of topics covered, the most useful for this program are Cities, Natural Wonders, and Monuments. Browse these categories and ask participants to tap a topic to learn more about. The topics contain maps, photos, audio clips, and short articles to explore. Swipe to the left to see all the media, or advance with the slide ribbon along the bottom of the screen. Tap the +Q icon on the bottom menu to see related topics. Tap the back icon to return to the previous topic, or search the database via the search bar in the upper right.

UN Country Stats is a powerful app for geographical and geopolitical information. From the main menu, select countries for an alphabetical list of countries with an image of their flag and region of the world.

1. Tap any country to reveal a data set covering population and area data and economic indicators.
2. Next, tap "Compare." This feature makes graphs comparing various countries among a variety of indicators. Direct students to tap "Add Countries" and pick three: China, India, and the United States. (Three is the limit.)
3. Next, tap "Change indicator." First, try "Tourist arrivals at national borders." Tap the orange "Show graph" button to build a graph on the right side of the screen. Which of the three

From *iPads in the Library: Using Tablet Technology to Enhance Programs for All Ages* by Joel A. Nichols. Santa Barbara, CA: Libraries Unlimited. Copyright © 2013.

countries has the highest numbers of tourists? Which has seen the biggest increase over the years shown?

4. Next, tap "Change indicator" again. Choose "Threatened species" and tap "Show graph." Which country has the most threatened species residing in it? Does the fact that it is the United States surprise you? Why or why not?

5. Next, tap "Change indicator" and chose "Internet users." Is it surprising that we have so many more Internet users than China, even though so many more people live there? Why or why not?

3D Cell Stain is an invaluable resource for the very specific homework assignment of learning the parts of a cell or making a cell model. It is a three-dimensional model of a cell that users can rotate with their fingertips and pinch in and out to zoom.

1. Tap the "Structure" icon along the left-hand side to view a still diagram with labels. Tap on any label to access a brief article explaining the structure and a stained photograph. There are also 13 short microscopic videos of cells in action.

2. Tap "Stain your own cell" for users to practice staining real microscope images of cell structures.

Users can stain up to four different structures.

Demonstrate **Merriam Webster HD** and **Science Glossary** briefly, perhaps asking participants to look up a word they were unfamiliar in either **3D Cell Stain** or **UN Country Stats**. Ask them which of these resources they like better, or which they should use for what kind of word.

Point out that **Merriam Webster HD** has a pronunciation option, so users can hear how a word sounds.

1. Tap the red speaker icon near the word.

2. Tap the microphone icon next to the search box to search a word by voice. Speak directly into the microphone. How does it do with recognizing your voice?

Figure 4.3
WhirlyGlobe offers an engaging and interactive map interface for learning about international and state borders.

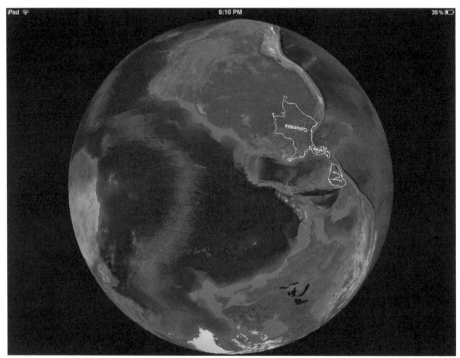

Screenshot courtesy Mousebird Consulting.

Goals: To introduce children to some basic map forms and to practice map skills.

Apps: Google Earth, WhirlyGlobe, Safari, Compass, Photo Roll

Planning Notes: Use **Safari** to browse for examples of very old maps, or use examples from books in your collection. Save any clear examples of old or ancient maps that demonstrate their hand-drawn character to the photo roll of the iPad.

Books/Other Materials: Set out a globe and atlases, to show examples, as well as any larger flat maps if you have them in your collection.

Instructions:
Start by asking basic questions about maps and about kinds of maps, referring to the globe, atlases, and flat maps that you have set out.

From *iPads in the Library: Using Tablet Technology to Enhance Programs for All Ages* by Joel A. Nichols.
Santa Barbara, CA: Libraries Unlimited. Copyright © 2013.

Ask participants to think about how maps are made. Did someone walk all over the world, tracing their steps? Did someone fly very high in a plane to get a "bird's-eye" view? What about before there were planes or balloon technology?

1. Open **Google Earth**. Turn on location services to zoom in your location. Demonstrate how to show the layers of the map: satellite, streets, traffic.
2. Explain and show each layer, being sure to hit these points: **Google Earth** was created with satellites as well as cameras on the ground. Satellites use cameras in space to make pictures; streets view shows a similar from-above image, but are drawn in computers; traffic puts a different kind of information on either of the other two maps.
3. Ask the participants to:
   a. Find their home address (or perhaps school address) map
   b. Find the library's address on the map
   c. Examine the driving directions, walking directions, and the public transportation directions on a route between the two addresses they chose. How do all three differ in terms of exact route, time, and distance? Do you actually use any of the ways shown to travel to and from the library?
   d. Change from satellite to traffic to streets view. What do these different views tell us about the area? Why would you use each?
4. Open **Atlas of the World**. This app features a simple home screen with three options: World, North America, and Landmarks. Each map features standard (political) view, satellite view, and a hybrid view. The World map features population data for each country, and is completely zoomable.
5. Tap North America to see population data for the United States, zoomable to the state level.
   Landmarks feature important buildings and features around the world, 260 in all, with extensive informational articles about the landmark and satellite images of it. Use the place finder icon in the upper right-hand corner of the screen to show all available landmarks, in order to pick one of particular interest to your users. From the Eiffel Tower to Macchu Picchu, the Hagia Sophia to the Golden Gate Bridge, there are many options, including natural features like Waterfalls.
6. Ask students to find a given landmark, such as the Grand Canyon or the Great Wall of China, and read the informational article as needed. Ask them to use the map and satellite image. What visual information can they see in the aerial photo that confirms what they read in the article? Participants can also switch back to **Google Earth** to plot a course from their hometown to one of these landmarks.
7. Have students find your state or territory. Ask them, which states or territories border yours? Do any other countries? Which of these states, territories, or countries has the largest population? (Note that the current version only has population data for U.S. States.) Discuss for a few moments, then switch to **WhirlyGlobe**.
8. Ask users to experiment with **WhirlyGlobe**, spinning the globe, turning on the country labels (with a single tap) and changing the size and zoom of the image through pinching in and out.
9. Play with this app for a few minutes. Can you figure out how to turn the country labels on and off? What about the borders of geographical features? What are some of the reasons to display a map like this as a globe instead of a flat map?

CARTOON CREATORS

Figure 4.4
PuppetPals HD lets children create and record their own digital puppet show.

Screenshot courtesy Polished Play LLC.

Goal: Have children create and produce their own cartoon puppet show, practicing elements of plot and structure by reading and retelling a story.

App: PuppetPals HD

Planning Notes: Introduce the group to the three simple parts of every story: beginning, or "problem"; middle, or "plot"; and the end, or "solution." Ask participants to tell you the beginning, middle, and end of any classic story or fairy tale (anything from *The Three Little Pigs* to *The Wizard of Oz*) that everyone might know. Ask them these questions:

- Who is the main character? (beginning)
- What is his/her/its main problem? (beginning)
- What are the things he/she/it does to solve the problem (plot/middle)
- How does the story end? (end)

Books/Other Materials: Familiar folktales such as *The Three Little Pigs* or *The Little Red Hen*; 3 x 3 square storyboard (made by dividing one sheet of paper into nine squares).

From *iPads in the Library: Using Tablet Technology to Enhance Programs for All Ages* by Joel A. Nichols.
Santa Barbara, CA: Libraries Unlimited. Copyright © 2013.

Instructions:

Read a folktale aloud. Ask the audience to think about what they think are the key movements in the story to bring it from beginning (problem) through the middle to the end (solution). Show pictures—on the iPad, or on photocopies—of the characters available in the app.

Hand out a 3 x 3 storyboard and ask the following questions:

- Where is your character? Use the first square to show us where your story is taking place. Remind them of some of the characters and backgrounds available in **Puppet Pals HD**. Show them the options on the iPad.
- What does your character need? Use squares 2 through 4 or 5 to show what your character needs. It can be a serious need, a funny need, or something else.
- And, for Square 5: what will your character do to find the thing she/he/it seeks?

1. Tap Start. Select characters from the next screen. Then tap "Next." Select a background. Users can select more than one background, and then swap them during the animation. Resize the backgrounds and the characters for maximum field of play. Pinch the characters, and use the slider bar for the background. When the objects are small and the background large, it is easier to move the objects around without running out of space.
2. Have students practice the narration/voice-over and the animation separately at least once each before trying them both together. It may work better to team up with a partner, with one person responsible for the animation and the other responsible for the voice-over and noises.
3. Tap the red record icon. To stop recording, press the square button. Then press play to see the cartoon you have created. From the home screen, tap "Export" to save to the Photo Roll or upload to YouTube.

LEGO SELF-PORTRAITS

Goal: Encourage children to experiment with and make a series of self-portraits using physical and digital tools.

Apps: Lego Photo, Photobooth, Toy Blocks

Books/Other Materials: *Matthew's Dream* by Leo Lionni or *Uncle Andy's Cats* by James Warhola; scrap paper and crayons; examples of self-portraits by a variety of artists such as Picasso, Kahlo, or Warhol—consider delivering these both electronically, via the **Safari** app, and with related books from the collection; Legos or other blocks (optional).

Instructions:
Welcome everyone to the program and then read the selected picture book. Show examples of self-portraits from those you have gathered. Ask participants to compare and contrast the examples.

Then hand out the paper and crayons. Ask everyone to draw a three-minute self-portrait. Remind them to use any colors they want and to imagine themselves in their ideal setting for the portrait. Collect the crayons and hand out the iPads.

1. Open **Photobooth**. There are nine photo distortion options to chose from. Be sure the rear facing camera is enabled. To do this, select one of the photo effects by tapping on it. Then look for the camera reverse icon in the lower right. Chose the desired effect by pressing the shutter icon on the lower left.
2. Encourage participants to photograph their paper self-portraits using all nine of the effects. They are: stretch, twirl, squeeze, light tunnel, normal, kaleidoscope, X-ray, mirror, and thermal camera. Have participants take some photographs of their faces, too.
3. Ask them to pay special attention to the thermal camera option. Are those the colors they would have picked for themselves? Why or why not?
4. Next, open **Lego Camera**. This simple app makes any photo into a mosaic made of Lego blocks. Note that it is an iPhone app, so you can use it magnified with a loss of resolution, or at half-size.
5. Select the camera button to use the in-app camera. Or, direct them to tap the Lego head icon to import a photo from the camera roll or photo stream. Participants can pick one of the self-portraits they just made in **Photobooth**.
6. When the photo imports, simply tap the image. It will refresh with a Lego tile mosaic. Tap it again to refresh with different colored tiles.
7. To save these images, tap the "i" icon in the upper right corner, and then tap "Save."

Encourage participants to use the in-app camera to take a photograph of the self-portrait they drew with crayons at the beginning of the program. What do they notice about their self-portrait the more they modify and experiment with it? Which styles do they like, and why? Which styles are most surprising? Do they look like themselves in all the portraits?

From *iPads in the Library: Using Tablet Technology to Enhance Programs for All Ages* by Joel A. Nichols. Santa Barbara, CA: Libraries Unlimited. Copyright © 2013.

With more advanced users or older children, consider using **Toy Blocks.** This is a three-dimensional block-building space where participants position blocks of different colors in three dimensions and build shapes. The build space is a grid that rotates in every direction. Scroll up and down and side to side with your fingertips to rotate it. Pinch in and out to move closer to and farther away from the build space.

The bottom row of navigation has just four options, and you will use three of these in this program. The colored square selects block style. Solid colors come only in the free version, but they are sufficient and even preferred for this program. To change the block color, tap the colored square and select a new color from the pop-up menu. The gestures in this app include a flick. Tap the settings icon and then the question mark icon to access the brief tutorial screen to explain all of the multitouch gestures used in this app.

1. Place a block by touching an empty square on the grid, and then by touching one side of the block. To remove a block, touch it and quickly flick your finger. These precise finger movements register better if the iPad screens are very clean. Zoom out as your structure or object gets better for a clearer view. Zoom in to remove blocks precisely.
2. Take screenshots by tapping the camera icon in the lower right.
3. Challenge users to recreate their Lego photo with these blocks, either as a mosaic, or to build a three-dimensional self-portrait using these blocks.

If available, or if there are not enough iPads to go around, have physical Legos on hand as an alternative medium.

ILLUSTRATED ACROSTIC

Goal: In this program, students will write and illustrate an acrostic poem using photographs.

Apps: Pic Stitch, Camera, Safari

An acrostic poem uses one word (or a name) typeset in one direction, with other words that describe the main word starting with each letter. For example:

> *Moon*
> Midnight's only light.
> October hauntings.
> Orbiting the Earth,
> Night after night.

Any word will work, and younger children might have an easier time with their own names if those names are short enough.

For the purposes of this program, stretch the literal meaning of acrostic, and let participants know that they will make a special kind of picture poem that is not necessarily laid out rigidly on an X-Y axis like a traditional acrostic. This adaptation opens up the options in **Pic Stitch** and allows participants more freedom for creativity.

Give them 10 minutes to choose a word and write their acrostic. Encourage students to pick words or names with only four or five letters.

Pic Stitch is an app that uses preset layout templates and photo editing options to make photo collages.

1. Tap the app to open and you will see up to 32 different layout grids to choose from. Each square in the layouts will have its own picture, and most of these layouts have only three, four, or five rectangles available.
2. Swipe to the left to page through the template grids. Select one by tapping it. There is no in-app camera in **Pic Stitch**. Instead, instruct participants to switch to the camera apps to take pictures for their illustration. Users can also search the Web for images via the **Safari** app.
3. If using images from the internet via **Safari**, press and hold on the image. A menu will pop up. Select "Save image," and it will automatically go to your camera roll.
4. Switch back to **Pic Stitch**. Double tap one of the rectangles on the grid, and select photo stream or camera roll to import the photos.
5. This opens the photo editor. As you see, there are many options to enhance, rotate, crop, change brightness, adjust contrast and saturation, fix blemishes, and so on.
6. For the purposes of this program, students will use mostly the Text icon. Select it and a transparent text box will appear over the image. Show them this, but note that they should fill in the pictures first.
7. Import photos into all the layout grids. Remind them to choose the placement of the pictures based on where their letters will go.
8. Return to each photo individually and add text boxes. Each picture should have one text box containing the word or sentence that makes up the poem. At least one of the grids will have two text boxes, one for the poem phrase and one for the original word.

From *iPads in the Library: Using Tablet Technology to Enhance Programs for All Ages* by Joel A. Nichols. Santa Barbara, CA: Libraries Unlimited. Copyright © 2013.

9. Type in the words you want and tap "Done" on the keyboard. Then move the text box to the desired location.

10. At this point, you can change the text color from the palette menu along the bottom navigation, and pull out and move the lower right-hand corner of the text box to enlarge, reduce, or rotate the text. (There is a gray circle on that corner of the box to mark where to pull and swipe.)

11. Tap "Apply" in the upper right to return to the photo editing page, and then "Done" in the same position to return to the main layout grid.

12. Gently move the photo around using your fingertip within that layout grid to adjust placement and make sure your text box is not cropped out or beyond the view of the frame.

13. Repeat until each grid has a photo and accompanying text. The main layout grid has a menu of five options along the bottom. *Layout* returns to other grid options to change the number and position of the rectangles. *Edit* accesses the photo editing menu (also accessed via double tap on an individual frame). *Aspect* transforms the dimensions of the overall project, offering many different sizes and ratios; if you plan to print these out, use 8 x 10 or 10 x 8. The *Color* icon offers three modes: full color, sepia, and black and white. Finally, *Export* allows users to email the collage, post it directly to Facebook, save it to the photo album, or open it in another image-editing program.

14. Export to save for printing or posting. For an advanced challenge, remind students that they could make a more complex **Pic Stitch** by making four different collages, and then using this app to stitch them all together into a bigger collage.

ANIMATED NAME VIDEO

Goal: To have elementary schoolchildren create a film in which animated toothpicks arrange themselves in the shape of letters, thereby learning simple video animation technique and reinforcing letter knowledge.

App: iMotion HD

Planning Notes: If there is not enough time to animate a whole name, consider having the children pick just one letter to make. Ahead of time, make a sample stop-motion with toothpicks. Use the following instructions. Note that if you do not already have a cover or stand for your iPad, or you need to make one for this activity. Make an excellent and simple stand using duct tape and a large metal bookend that will keep the iPad camera pointed at the right angle. Be sure to avoid the camera lens when affixing the tape.

Figure 4.5
Use a bookend and a few pieces of tape to make a sturdy and temporary tripod for the iPad.

Photo by Joel A. Nichols

From *iPads in the Library: Using Tablet Technology to Enhance Programs for All Ages* by Joel A. Nichols. Santa Barbara, CA: Libraries Unlimited. Copyright © 2013.

Figure 4.6

When taping the edges and lining up the camera, be sure you do not obscure the cameras themselves or any part of the multitouch interface your audience will need for the program.

Photo by Joel A. Nichols

Books/Other Materials: Toothpicks, or other objects to animate

Instructions:

Explain how stop animation is made, by taking many still photographs and moving the objects in between each frame. Show your example. Explain that everyone is going to create their name out of toothpicks. Hand out the toothpicks. Demonstrate how to bend and break them to create rounder shapes, and direct everyone to start making their names out of toothpicks. Participants can also construct block letters without having to break the toothpicks.

Once they have made their name, have them remove the toothpicks one by one, taking a photo in between each toothpick move. They can also move the toothpicks slightly in between each shot to simulate them crawling away, rather than just disappearing.

1. Open **iMotion HD**. Tap "New Movie" to access the screen to set up your clip. Fill in a title in that field. This app allows remote access for time-lapse photography. Ignore the options "Time-lapse" and "Remoted" for now. Tap "Manual" and then "Start."
2. While this app can capture sound with the microphone, this program works better filming silent clips and then setting them to music later.
3. Use the "Options" button. Select "Grid" and "Onion Skin" to turn on these options. Grid superimposes green directional lines over the image on the display for precise line-up. Onion skin ghosts the previous image in over the display so users can control the exact amount of movement per frame.
4. Start filming! Tap "Capture." Slightly move the toothpicks. It will be easier for participants to move all the toothpicks in every frame. Tap "Capture." Repeat. This process is laborious, but let them know that this is where all the interesting visuals happen. Students should slowly, frame by frame, move the toothpicks around on the screen until they are in the shape of their names.
5. Do not worry about frames that capture a stray hand or finger, or that are errors. Users can delete individual frames in postproduction.
6. When all the frames have been captured, tap stop to start postproduction.
7. Use the slider bar to set the desired rate of frames per second. Lower numbers of frames per second correspond to slower animation.
8. Use the Tools menu to advance frame by frame. Use the Pause button to freeze a frame, and then tap the delete icon on the far right to delete it.
9. To resume capturing frames, return to the home screen. Tap "My Movies," and then tap "Resume" on the movie you want to edit.
10. Or, tap export to save this film to your photo roll or to Facebook. From the photo library, this movie can be exported or emailed.

CLIMATE (AFTERSCHOOL SCIENCE)

Goal: Students learn how to access and interpret different kinds of climate and weather information.

Apps: Vestas Weather, EarthObserver, Greenpeace Images, Safari, Merriam Webster HD

Instructions: Start this program with **Merriam Webster HD**. Look up the difference between the terms climate and weather. (You can also use paper dictionaries from your collection!)

EarthObserver has World, Arctic, and Antarctic views. In each map view, you can toggle between a base map (the default) and a range of other options. Start in the World view, and tap the filters for Snow, Ice, and Water. Select "Ice Cover" and ask students to study the following features of the map: the legend in the upper left corner with a colored scale representing the percentage of sea ice, as well as color codes for dry snow and permanent ice sheets.

Be sure to encourage students to zoom in and out by pinching the map. In the Antarctic view, map options to choose include: Earthquakes, Sea Ice Concentration, Sea Ice Extent, and so on. The objective here is to observe changes in Sea Ice throughout the year in Antarctica and the Arctic. Prompt participants to chose "Sea Ice Concentration." Students will be able to see gradations in sea ice concentration easily on this map, shaded from icy white to dark blue.

Ask participants to make a short chart with the following values for both the Arctic and Antarctic:

Sea Ice Concentration—January—Arctic
Sea Ice Concentration—July—Arctic
Sea Ice Concentration—January—Antarctic
Sea Ice Concentration—July—Antarctic

Participants will quickly see that the Arctic July and Antarctic January show the lowest values of ice concentration. Ask them why the data matches up this way.

Be sure to point out that the differences between seasons in the Northern and Southern Hemispheres are shown on the map, using ice concentration mapped to specific geolocations.

Remind them that they have been using climate information, and turn them toward the next app, **Vestas Weather**. This app feeds real-time weather data to an interactive map. Note that this app in its current form is optimized for the iPhone, so you have to use it magnified and at a lower resolution.

Examine the weather at your location, by selecting "Map" on the bottom menu, and then picking three data options: current temperature, current wind speed, and current weather types. Ask participants to think about the following questions:

From *iPads in the Library: Using Tablet Technology to Enhance Programs for All Ages* by Joel A. Nichols. Santa Barbara, CA: Libraries Unlimited. Copyright © 2013.

1. Compare the current month of actual weather data (in **Vestas Weather**) with the same month of Arctic/Antarctic data. Do you see any current patterns that match up to or contradict the climate map?
2. What are the most important features of the climate where they live? What is the temperature like on a daily basis this week?

Now make a climate closet drawing. Pass out blank paper and ask participants to pick a season—you can pick the current season in your area, or pick something older students could check against the climate maps (January in Johannesburg, South Africa, or August in Kiev, Ukraine, etc.).

Encourage everyone to draw the three or four pieces of clothing they would need in whatever climate they chose.

End the program by using **Greenpeace Images** to show images of actual Arctic climate science. When the app opens, swipe the welcome image to the right to find the pictures of the *Arctic Sunrise*, a Greenpeace ship on expedition in the Arctic. You can also use a navigation icon located to the right of the play button icon to find access to these images. There is a series of six photographs with captions showing Arctic climate science in action to help illustrate some of these concepts in a different modality.

THE MOON

Goal: Teach participants how to observe the moon from Earth and about its phases and rotational pattern.

Apps: Moon Globe, NASA Visualizer, YouTube or Safari

Planning Notes: Find animations of the moon, the sun, and the earth rotating online through via the YouTube app.

Books/Other Materials: *Faces of the Moon* by Bob Crelin; *When the Moon is Full: A Lunar Year* by Penny Pollock (poems); *The Moon by Seymour Simon*, *The Way Back Home* (fiction picture book) by Oliver Jeffers; "Neil Armstrong the First Man Walking on the Moon" panorama, accessed at http://www.photojpl.com (or Google, "Neil Armstrong the First Man Walking on the Moon panorama"); International Observe the Moon Night's activity kit accessed at http://observethemoonnight.org (or Google, "observe the moon night activities"). Also round sandwich cookies (such as Oreos) and craft sticks or plastic knives.

Instructions:

Start this program by reading a book about the moon to the group. Chose easy nonfiction or a folktale/picture book from the options above.

Ask participants what they already know about the moon. You want to write some of their answers on a whiteboard if your room allows it. What is it made out of? Why does it appear to change shape throughout the month? What does the expression "once in a blue moon" mean?

Tell participants that they are going to see why the moon changes shape because of where it is located relative to the earth and the sun.

Use **YouTube or Safari** to find and show an animated model of the moon, the earth, and the sun rotating. The best ones show both the phase of the moon and the relative positions of all three bodies. Play these animations several times, and consider doing an additional activity you can find in the International Observe the Moon Night Kit where participants, in small groups, use their bodies and a powerful flashlight to act out the rotation of the moon.

1. Open the **NASA HD** app and direct participants to look at the moon in the context of the solar system. Remind participants that this visualization is not in scale, and that the earth and moon are far smaller than they appear here. Also remind them that many of the other planets in our solar system are also orbited by moons.

2. Tap on the moon itself to open up a page with reference data about the moon, including the average distance from the earth as well as the radius, circumference, mass, density, length of day, surface temperatures, etc. Point out any information you want participants to know from this article, or ask them to swipe to the bottom of the page to show important dates in the history of humans learning about the moon. This helps show the different scientific methods used over time to observe and understand the moon.

3. Now, open **Moon Globe**. The app includes a tutorial screen with very useful and specific information, which will run the first time you launch the app if you tap "How to Use Moon Globe," and which is accessible by tapping the question mark icon on the top navigation ribbon.

4. Ask students to rotate the Moon globe, and demonstrate how to zoom in and out by pinching. Tap the Terrain icon on the top left of the navigation ribbon and show them how to turn the Terrain (geographic names) and Spacecraft landing site label names on and off. The next icon to the right on the navigation ribbon displays a menu with more details for both of these data sets, and make it easy to zoom in on a specific terrain feature with its location on the surface of the moon.

5. Next, tap the Globe icon in the upper left of the screen and tap viewpoint to change the view from a globe to telescope view. This shows how the same part of the moon is always facing the earth.

6. Tap the Time icon shaped like a clock on the upper right. This will enable a light slider in the upper right corner of the screen. As it moves from full sun to full dark, the corresponding slice of moon is illuminated. Ask participants to connect this to their viewing experience. Are the darker parts of the moon ever visible during a New or Quarter Moon? Why or why not? What are some of the conditions that make it easier or harder to see the phases of the moon?

7. Ask participants to model and name each phase of the moon using this slider bar. To refresh and reinforce their knowledge about the relative positions of the earth, sun, and moon, direct them to tap the compass icon on the top left, which will show the relative positions of the moon and the sun from the earth.

8. Hand out the sandwich cookies, split them in half, and have participants make models of each phase of the moon by scraping off the appropriate amount (half or quarter) of the frosting with the plastic knives. Eat the rest.

To extend this program, access the panoramic surface photography taken of Neil Armstrong's walk accessible at via Google search described above. Ask participants to find that exact location on the Moon globe. Compare the images side by side on two iPads: are there any differences in these images?

GRAPHING POLLUTION

Goal: To introduce participants to current trends in the environment, including carbon footprints, local pollution, and international trends. This is perfect as an extender to a science program about climate or as a program to celebrate Earth Day.

Apps: Greenpeace Images, Pollution App, Planets, China Air Pollution Index (CN Air Quality), CO2 Emissions Calculator, Tuna in Trouble, Safari, Pages

Planning Notes: Find a current news article about air pollution or water contamination.

Books/Other Materials: *Mama Miti: Wangari Maathai and the Trees of Kenya* by Donna Jo Napoli.

Instructions:
Start by saying, "Pollution is one way of measuring the human impact on the environment. So is energy consumption. This program will show some examples of measuring this human impact."

1. In **Planets**: Use Globe view by tapping on the globe icon at the bottom of the screen. It displays an interactive globe of the earth showing, in real time, which parts of the earth are currently dark and which are light. Spin the globe slower until you can see the parts of the earth where it is night, and zoom in until the resolution becomes fuzzy. (This globe is only interactive to the level of continents.)
2. Remind participants that these images are taken from space. What do they notice about the brightest spots? Where are they? Where are the darkest spots at night? The information on this globe can show where there is greater light pollution, and can show how much energy is used during the night—and during the day, powering air conditioning and electronics—in these hot spots around the world. Ask participants, "How does your location compare to other places on Earth?"
3. Next, use **Pollution App**. This app uses your current location within a selected radius to show possible sources of air, water, ground, and radio-wave pollution. Note that this is an app designed for the iPhone, so you should magnify it on the iPad screen although there is a slight loss of resolution.
4. Direct participants to pick a radius around your current location, or use the default of 30 km. This option is located inside the Settings menu, accessed by tapping on the icon at the bottom of the screen. The built-in map shows each possible source of pollution. Each source has a different icon based on type.
5. Use **Pages** to make a chart of this data. Open a new document by tapping the plus sign in the upper left corner. Then tap the insert button (also shaped like a plus sign icon) on the upper right of the document menu. Chose Charts, and then chose between the preset design options in 2D and 3D. There are options for bar graphs, pie charts, and line graphs.
6. Once the chosen chart template is inserted into the document, tap on it and then chose the "Edit data" button that pops up. Participants can quickly plug in the four pollution

types—air, water, ground or radio waves—into one axis and the total numbers from their search into the other. Remember to use the five-finger swipe to switch between apps.

7. Participants can take a screenshot of this graph by pressing the home and shut off buttons simultaneously. If desired, these screenshots could be posted online, emailed, or printed as a takeaway from this program.

8. Ask participants to compare the kinds of pollution in their community? Which kind—air, water, ground or radio waves—is most prevalent? Is this surprising? Do they recognize the names of the sites or companies listed in the results?

Next, turn to **China Air Pollution Index**, an app with real-time air quality data for China. Note that students may want to compare these data to what they find for their own city or area in **Pollution App**. If desired, encourage them to make these comparisons.

  China Air Pollution Index shows trends in air quality over time in China, allowing users to use short and long time spans with one tap, from 1 day to 3.

1. There are six cities to choose from on the bottom navigation, or you can direct participants to choose cities from the map.

2. From here, participants could make a graph of comparing air pollution numbers between two or more Chinese cities. Or, direct them to compare this map to the map of light hot spots they viewed in **Planets**. Is it brighter where there is worse air quality?

(Hint: depending on your time zone, you may need to artificially change the time to make these Chinese cities show up in the dark. Tap the options icon on the bottom navigation, then switch Automatic Date & Time to off. Then switch the Time from AM to PM, which should do the trick.)

  More advanced participants could also return to Pollution App and expand the radius to include more area, and then use the light pollution map in **Planets** to see if there is a brightness/pollution source correlation in their own communities.

  Another activity to expand and extend this program is using the **CO2 Emissions Calculator**, which gives carbon data for flights. Pick an origin and a destination airport. The following data is reported: average fuel burned on this route, average number of seats per flight, average CO2 per passenger, and distance. These additional data can be used to populate more graphs or charts, either on paper or using **Pages**.

  A fun way to end this program is with two Greenpeace Apps. First, open **Greenpeace Images** and allow participants to explore contemporary environmental activism and education through series of annotated photographs that are vivid and captivating on the iPad's bright display. Second, use **Tuna in Trouble**, a game designed to show the hazards of industrial fishing. The goal is for the tuna to swim through the net rather than to crash into it. This game will be a hit with younger participants up to age 10. It uses the on-board accelerometer to navigate. This means that users will need to hold the device in both hands. They control the tuna by moving the device right and left and tilting in forward and backward. There are two levels in the free version, which are enough to end the program.

Figure 4.7

The wide variety of pollution data in **China Air Pollution Index** gives your students plenty of data points to chart and compare.

Screenshot courtesy Fresh-Ideas Studio.

INTRODUCTION TO THE SOLAR SYSTEM

Goals: To introduce participants to the planets and other major features of our solar system, demonstrate the scale of the planets and their size relative to humans, and to expose participants to what features of the solar system they can observe from Earth.

Apps: NASA HD, Planets, Mars Globe, Camera

Instructions:
First, make a list of all the planets everyone can name. Then, ask them to name other things they might find on a trip through our solar system, including asteroids, comets, and so forth.

1. Open **NASA HD** and orient participants to this atlas of the solar system, showing the sun, and the planets, as well as links to further information about other topics: asteroids, comets, meteors, and the universe. Tap the links for these options to show examples of the reference pages in this app. Each planet has a page of information like this if participants want to look up specifics about any of the planetary bodies discussed in this program.

2. Remind them that these bodies are enormous, compared to our human scale, and that the distances between them are very far. Remind them that it takes months and years to even reach Mars and Venus, the closest planets to Earth. Tap the "Featured" button on the bottom navigation menu. Then select "Scale of the Solar System." This informational graphic shows two visualizations of the planets on top of each other. Along the bottom, it shows the planets in their correct relative orbital distances, and along the top planets are shown in correct relative size to each other.

3. Ask users some or all of the following questions:
   - Which planets are the largest?
   - Which are the farthest from the sun?
   - Is Saturn closer to the sun than it is to Uranus or Neptune?

4. Ask participants to discuss anything that surprises them about these distances or these sizes.

5. Next, open **Planets**. Tap the Sky 3D icon to display an interactive 3D map of the sky showing the positions of planets and constellations in the visible hemisphere relative to where we are on Earth. Note that the map also rotates to show the nonvisible hemisphere, which is shaded green.

6. Challenge participants to find as many of the planets as they can. Are they all visible in our hemisphere? Which ones are only visible in the sky of the other hemisphere right now?

   Ask participants which, if any, of the planets they have observed on their own. Then tap the "Visibility" icon in the center of the bottom navigation menu. This offers a chart of each planet, the moon, and the sun, and when they are visible from Earth. Note that Uranus and Neptune are not visible to the unaided eye.

7. Next, access video content from within the app to explain why Pluto is not a planet. Tap options on the lower right of the menu and then tap "Why Pluto Is Not a Planet," which will load a YouTube video explaining the planetary science behind this designation. You can also

From *iPads in the Library: Using Tablet Technology to Enhance Programs for All Ages* by Joel A. Nichols.
Santa Barbara, CA: Libraries Unlimited. Copyright © 2013.

read a picture book on the same topic, such as *When Is a Planet Not a Planet: The Story of Pluto* by Elaine Scott.

End this program by asking each participant to pick a planet they want to make a model of. These will be informational models. These models could be actual models out of clay or Styrofoam balls, or they could be simply drawings on paper that capture the given planet's colors and features. Ask students to pick the five most important facts about their chosen planet to include on their informational model. If you use clay or Styrofoam balls, students can display their facts by clipping an index card to a paper clip, and then unbending one piece to stick into their model. Students should spend 10–15 minutes researching their planets in **Planets** and **NASA HD** to come up with the five most important things. They could also pick comets or asteroids to research.

Use the **Camera** app to document the models to share on the library's website and social media presences.

5

Teen Programs

DIGITAL STORYTELLING AND HOMAGO
(HANGING OUT, MESSING AROUND, AND GEEKING OUT)

Hanging Out, Messing Around, and Geeking Out (HoMaGo) is a phrase coined by Professor Mizuko Ito, and refers to modes of learning in the new media.[1] It is a catchall term that describes what happens when young people have access to and mentorship about new media and digital tools. It deemphasizes structured programs like the ones described here in favor of mentor-led but ultimately free-form exploration of tools and experimentation with content creation. Any of the programs outlined in this book could become the basis of an effective HoMaGo session, because these programs teach users media creation skills and give them time to practice them. These plans can also help mentors learn the basics as they begin to mentor young people experimenting with media creation.

Digital Storytelling is a generic term that encompasses all forms of computer-aided media production and participatory media production. It is a way to translate the stories we are used to reading in books into stories that are told and heard, produced and consumed with digital tools. It encompasses media beyond (but also including) text: voice, sound, photo, image, and video, sometimes mixed together and sometimes not. Examples include podcasts, photo slideshows, blog posts, hypertext novels, animated GIFs, and so on. Any digital media tool that can convey narrative should be put in the service of this kind of storytelling.

Many of the programs detailed in this book for children and teens are digital storytelling programs. Librarians and teachers should adapt them for different kinds of content and different kinds of stories. While these programs are highly structured and organized, I have included many places to substitute and adapt based on different content or instructional needs.

If you want these programs to be more flexible and user-directed, please adapt them that way. Keep in mind the following tips:

1. *Use Samples and Examples*: Teens hanging out and geeking around will eventually produce interesting art and media projects. With limited programming time, guide their experimentation by showing them samples of work you have created with these same tools, as well as examples from their peers or from professional artists.

2. *Prompts*: Sometimes teens cannot "create on demand" and need inspiration. Prompts, though, can jump-start a story. Prompts could include interesting photographs or objects users are asked to describe (or talk or dance) about. They can also be structured writing exercises that ask participants to describe, using vivid language (or sounds or movements) three different textures: sticky, spongy, and coarse, for example. Highly artificial but specific situations like these can help writers start writing, even if they do not feel any creative spark at the moment. Use and adapt other creative writing prompts to strengthen these digital storytelling programs.

ELECTRONIC SHORT STORY WORKSHOP

Goal: To expose participants to a variety of creative writing prompts that encourage them to write a story based on a prompt.

Apps: Pages or another word processing app.

Planning Notes: This program would work well as part of a writing workshop series and could work as a virtual program as well, delivered completely online. If you have enough time, start by reading a short story or microfiction together at the beginning of every workshop. Take time to point out the fictional elements—setting, characterization, point of view, language, etc.—you want the students to notice.

Books/Other Materials: Some short stories to try with teens are: "Bloodchild" by Octavia Butler in *Bloodchild and Other Stories*; "Singing My Sister Down" or "Sweet Pippit" by Margo Lanagan in *Black Juice*; selections from *The Coyote Road: Trickster Tales*, edited by Ellen Datlow and Terri Windling, or *Welcome to Bordertown*, edited by Holly Black and Ellen Kushner.

Instructions:

1. Start with **Pages**. Tap the plus-sign icon to create a new blank document. Read several of the following writing prompts and allow participants three to five minutes after each to craft a paragraph of a story.
   - Describe a basketball without using the words round, orange, or ball
   - Describe an orange without using the words round, orange, or fruit
   - Tomorrow morning, you wake up to find a spaceship sitting in the street outside your house. Did it land? Did it crash? Was there anyone—or anything—on board? Write what happens next.
   - Dr. Barbara Boingboing, a mad scientist, is hiring a new lab assistant to work on her cybernetic frog project. Write the job ad she should post on the bulletin board in the lobby of the mad science building.
   - Two hundred years ago, one of your ancestors took a long trip somewhere. Who were they? Where did they live, and where did they go? How did they travel? How much did it cost?
   - Two hundred years from now, one of your descendants will take a long trip somewhere. Who will they be? Where will they travel? What method of transportation do you think they might take?
   - Describe these five smells using all five senses: gasoline, ice cream, peanut butter, a rainstorm, and the library.
   - You are a meteorologist on vacation when a huge hurricane hits the place you are visiting. Your network calls and asks you to give a live report of the storm. Describe what you can hear and see from your hotel room.

- Otto Oublious, a very forgetful person, just locked himself out of his house or apartment. What does he do next? Use this exercise to focus on setting: describe Otto's lock and door, Otto's street or yard, and so on.

2. After enough time has passed and participants have at least a paragraph or two of text, invite participants to share by reading aloud.

3. Ask them to continue writing a story based on this paragraph. For a one-time program, instruct them to keep it to no more than two paragraphs. If you are conducing this in a series of writing workshops, proceed to the next steps only when participants have a larger chunk of story produced to share.

StoryKit allows users to make and format their own eBooks. Open StoryKit and tap New Book. Tap the A+ icon to edit text on a new page. Users can compose text in this app, but it is easier to switch to **Pages** and select and copy what they have already written. Then switch back to **StoryKit** and press and hold your fingertip until the paste button appears. Tap it. Add new pages as needed. When all of the text is pasted in, users can add images from the Camera or from the **Photo Roll** or even sounds or drawings created by tapping the paintbrush icon to launch a simple line-drawing tool. The book will automatically be saved to the Bookshelf. From this main menu page, users can read their eBook, edit it more, or share it on StoryKit's server. To access the story online, users receive a weblink they can share on social media or with other participants.

CHOOSE YOUR OWN PATH ADVENTURE

Goal: To have teens write and construct a story with alternative actions, depending on the user picking among plot choices.

App: Keynote, **Pages**, or other word processing app

Planning Notes: Developing the storyline and alternates will take some time and creativity, especially with younger participants. Because of this relative complexity, this makes a great program for parents to do with a first through fourth grader, or for older tweens and teens working together.

Books/Other Materials: Paper storyboard, or storyboard app; *Choose Your Own Adventure* series books from your collection.

Instructions:

Make your own sample story following the template below. It will serve as an excellent example to get your students or participants thinking creatively about their story structure. Or, read a couple chapters of a *Choose Your Own Adventure* book from your collection.

This program achieves interactivity by leveraging **Keynote**'s functionality to create hyperlinks in slideshows. So instead of participants needing to proceed linearly through a slide deck, participants can link specific words and images on a slide to take users to any other slide. In this way, you can structure an interactive story that puts readers in the driver's seat.

1. Open **Keynote**. The app will open with one presentation already there to select, a presentation called Getting Started. This is an app tutorial—in presentation format—that users should review. It contains very specific help and a preview of **Keynote**'s most powerful features.
2. My sample story is called "This Is Moon Base." I will map out the first seven slides, which establishes a pattern and structure that you or users can follow to complete an entire story, or to make a short adventure that ends in seven slides.
3. For each slide, you can read the content and text on the slide and see which words/images/shapes are hyperlinked and to which other slide they link.
4. First, create these slides:

Slide 1
Text: "This is the moon. Do you want to land on the *light side* or the *dark side*?"
Picture: Picture of the moon from far away.

Slide 2
Text: "The dark side is cold. Do you have more *oxygen* or *water* with you in your supplies?"
Picture: Images representing air and water, picture of astronaut

From *iPads in the Library: Using Tablet Technology to Enhance Programs for All Ages* by Joel A. Nichols. Santa Barbara, CA: Libraries Unlimited. Copyright © 2013.

Slide 3

Text: "Uh-oh. You don't have enough energy to burn the water for heat. You freeze to death in 72 hours."

Picture: Arrow saying "Start over."

Slide 4

Text: "Good! You can breathe some of that air and burn some of it for heat. You can survive up to 100 hours, which gives you time to reach the Moon Base."

Picture: Use text or graphic that says "Proceed to the Moon Base."

Slide 5

Text: "Good! It's easier to stay alive on the light side, because it's warmer. Should you proceed to the Moon Base immediately or should you explore a really unique and unusual crater that will make you famous?"

Picture: Closeup of moon's surface.

Slide 6

Text: "Whoops! You fell off the edge of the crater."

Picture: Closeup of a crater; arrow saying "Start over."

Slide 7

Text: "Welcome to Moon Base Alpha. Wait, it seems as though the lights are all out. Should you break down the door with your moon axe, or should you walk around the other entrance airlock on the other side of the base?"

5. Once these slides are created, go back and add the hyperlinks detailed below. To add hyperlinks, tap the wrench icon, then tap the Advanced button. Select Interactive Hyperlinks, and a blue bar will appear across the top of the screen to show that you are in link mode. On each slide, tap the appropriate word or picture and then tap "link to slide" and chose the appropriate number slide.

Slide 1

Text: "This is the Moon. Do you want to land on the *light side* or the *dark side*?"

Picture: Picture of the Moon from far away.

Link "light side" to slide 5.

Link "dark side" to slide 2.

Slide 2

Text: "The dark side is cold. Do you have more *oxygen* or *water* with you in your supplies?"

Picture: Images representing air and water, picture of astronaut

Link "oxygen" to slide 4.

Link "water" to slide 3.

Slide 3

Text: "Uh-oh. You don't have enough energy to burn the water for heat. You freeze to death in 72 hours."

Picture: Arrow saying *"Start over."*

Link the arrow labeled "Start over" to slide 1.

Slide 4

Text: "Good! You can breathe some of that air and burn some of it for heat. You can survive up to 100 hours, which gives you time to reach the Moon Base."

Picture: Use text or graphic that says *"Proceed to the Moon Base."*

Link "Proceed to the Moon Base" text or graphic to slide 7.

Slide 5

Text: "Good! It's easier to stay alive on the light side, because it's warmer. Should you *proceed to the Moon Base immediately* or should you *explore a really unique and unusual crater* that will make you famous?"

Picture: Closeup of Moon's surface

Link "proceed to the Moon Base immediately" to slide 7.

Slide 6

Text: "Whoops! You fell off the edge of the crater."

Picture: Closeup of a crater; arrow saying "Start over."

Link the arrow labeled "Start over" to slide 1.

Slide 7

Text: "Welcome to Moon Base Alpha. Wait, it seems as though the lights are all out. Should you break down the door with your moon axe, or should you walk around the other entrance airlock on the other side of the base?"

And so on. To continue this story, for example, you could make a slide for each option identified in slide 7 (*"break down the door"* or *"check other entrance"*) and then link it appropriately.

Users can continue adding to this story or start making up their own. Remember that some plot options can have more than two choices, and that not all choices have to end with a dead end or starting the story over. Encourage participants to try out many different strategies. It is much easier create all of the slides first and then add the hyperlinks, so mapping this out on a paper storyboard is useful, as you will have noticed when making the sample described above.

Encourage users to use animations. In the story above, I would add a Lens Flare effect to the first photos, and a Flames effect for the "start over" arrows.

To add these effects, tap the first photo and select "build-in." This ensures that the effect will play at the beginning of the side. Then select Lens Flare, or any effect you like, from the menu, and click anywhere outside of the menu. Find the "start over" arrows on slides 3 and 6. Tap them and select animation. Select "build-out" so the effect will happen at the end of the slide. Then tap Flames, and tap anywhere outside the animations menu.

At the end of this program, users should read and play each other's interactive games, and export them as **Keynote** or PowerPoint files to share.

COMIC INSTRUCTIONS

Figure 5.1
Strip Designer's versatile layout and design options will captivate comic book fans and make it easy for teens to write and illustrate with heavy graphics.

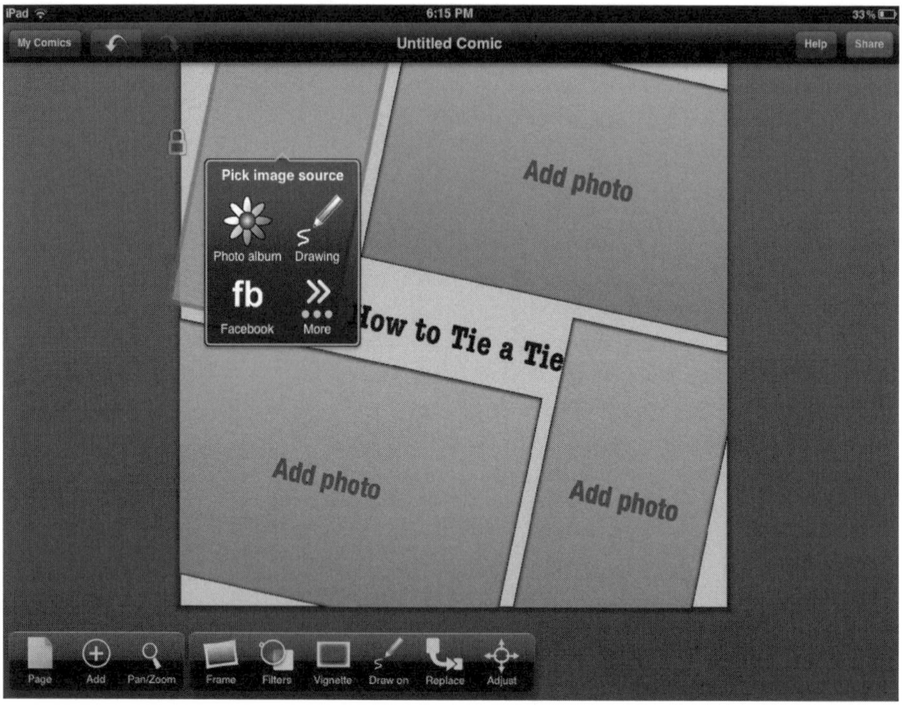

Screenshot courtesy Vivid Apps.

Goal: For participants to produce a set of any instructions for any process in comic-strip format.

Apps: Camera, Strip Designer

Planning Notes: Help participants identify a process to illustrate. Great examples are how to tie your shoes, how to tie a knot, how to do a pushup, how to braid hair, etc. It should be a simple process that is easy to illustrate and act out in the library.

Instructions:
Ask students to plan out their instructions by writing brief bullet points. They will use these bullet points like a shooting script, to keep their illustrations focused.

1. Open **Camera**. Take a series of pictures illustrating your instructions. Take several, and do not be afraid to be silly! They should aim to illustrate their strip with between four and eight photos.

From *iPads in the Library: Using Tablet Technology to Enhance Programs for All Ages* by Joel A. Nichols. Santa Barbara, CA: Libraries Unlimited. Copyright © 2013.

2. Open **Strip Designer**. Tap "Create New." A pop-up menu with several layout options will appear. Tap "Plain" for this program, but let participants know they can test out and preview the other layouts as well. Next, select a template for the individual panels of the strip with anywhere from one to four pictures.

3. If participants want to use up to eight photos, they can make a second strip to add to this first one of four by tapping Page on the bottom of the main workspace screen.

4. Next, tap "Add photo" to import the images from the photo roll. Tap the "Add" icon to add cells. These cells can either be more photos or more text boxes—this is a great way to add headlines. Tap "Balloon" to add speech or thought balloons in many shapes. Double-tap them to change the text. Single-tap them to move the balloons around. When editing these text balloons, users can change font, color, and balloon shape by tapping the icons along the bottom of the workspace. (*Hint*: the app comes with art in seven categories called "Stickers" that can be imported to a panel.) Finally, the "Warp Text" icon will add a large text banner that can be shaped on top of and around the photo cells.

5. When students are happy with their illustrated instructions, tap "Share." From this menu, users can tap settings to change resolution and file format (JPEG and PNG are available). This app has many export settings: emailing as a JPG or PDF, adding to the photo album or opening on the iPad as a PDF, as well as in-app links to Facebook, Twitpic, and Flickr. Users can also save the file and send their creations to the iTunes Store.

TWO-MINUTE MEMOIR

Goal: To record a produce a podcast or narrated slideshow. It works well as a short "memoir" because participants will find it easy to talk about the things they enjoy, their hobbies and friends, where they live, how they get to school, etc.

Apps: TellAStory, VoiceThread

Books/Other Materials: Stories or podcasts available as samples, via Stitcher or iTunes download.

Instructions:
Direct participants to take five minutes to plan out a story, and ask prompting questions such as these:

• What is your favorite thing to do on a relaxing Saturday?
• Who is the most important person in your life and why?
• Where do you see yourself in 10 years?
• What is the biggest change you would make if you could do anything?

At this point, if they chose the slideshow option, they will need time to gather images from the Internet, to take pictures of themselves or of things in the library (favorite books and movies), or from books.

For a sound-only podcast, use **TellAStory**. This no-frills app allows you to record a voice track, and then add effects or samples from two other tracks: sound effects included in the app and from the iPad music library.

1. Press "Record," and a timer starts to show your progress. Speak slowly, loudly, and clearly directly into the microphone for best results.
2. Press "Stop," and then save to end the recording and make it available in the editing deck. The audio just recorded will appear as a colored block on the top track in the editing deck.
3. The second editing track is for sound effects. The app is preloaded with a variety of sounds, from creaky doors to chirping crickets. Click on the category options (Reptiles, Insects, Animals, Birds, other) in the sound library to see the available effects.
4. Tap to select and import the sound. They will appear as green blocks.
5. The third editing track is to import a song from the music library, which appears as a blue block.
6. The scissor icon trims parts of the recording you want to delete. There are three icons that control the editing mode. Tap the hand icon to move the blocks around. Tap the "move-mode" icon to move and isolate selections of clip. Tap the delete ("x") icon to isolate and delete sections of the clip. Mix and remix!
7. Tap "Save," and export via email. To edit a project again, tap "Edit."

For the podcast with photos in a slideshow, use **VoiceThread**. First, import the pictures for the slideshow found online, or take some. Tap the green plus sign to import

From *iPads in the Library: Using Tablet Technology to Enhance Programs for All Ages* by Joel A. Nichols. Santa Barbara, CA: Libraries Unlimited. Copyright © 2013.

from the photo roll (library) or tap camera to take pictures from within the app. Select as many photos as needed. Tap "Done."

1. The pictures will appear in a row next to the green plus sign. Tap "Comment."
2. From this screen, choose what kind of narration to add. Tap the "ABC" bubble to add text to the image, tap the microphone bubble to record voice-over, and tap the videocamera bubble to create a picture-in-picture video of yourself delivering the voice-over.
3. Prompt participants to try all three. One nice feature is that audio and video options offer a countdown after participants press "Record," rather than starting automatically.
4. Swipe to the right to move to the next photo and add a comment. Repeat until each photo has comments.
5. Tap the envelope icon to share this **VoiceThread** via email. This email generates a link via which other participants can view and add comments to the **VoiceThread**.

A third app with which you can run this program is **Fotobabble**. Its interface and options are simple, and they will work well whether you adapt this program for an older or younger audience.

1. Open **Fotobabble**. Tap "Take new photo" to use the camera in the app, or the icon to the right of that to import images from the photo roll.
2. Tap the microphone icon to record and to stop recording, and swipe the photos to the left when you want to move to the next one.

This app has built-in photo tools accessed via tapping "Edit" at the bottom right of the photo. There are Instagram-like photo filters, as well as crop and rotation tools.

MY OWN PERSONAL RADIO

Goals: To connect teens with digital radio players that allow them to find the song and audio content they already love, and to discover new content.

Apps: Stitcher, Pandora, YouTube, or YouTube content delivered via **Safari**

Books/Other Materials: Headphones for each teen, if desired.

Instructions:
First, ask participants to find their favorite song or artist on **YouTube**. Show them how to look for and watch related videos. Tap "More videos from this user" to browse for more content. Ask participants if this is how they find and consume their favorite content already. If not, ask them to demonstrate how they search and browse YouTube.

1. Open **Pandora**. This app builds custom song lists based on user input. So when users enter their favorite band or singer, **Pandora** might not—because of rights and permissions—play that particular artist. But it will play similar kinds of music. Usually, the specific, desired artist does also show up.
2. Open **Stitcher**. This app delivers all kinds of radio and podcast content. Users can search for their favorite radio stations and radio shows, or they can use the search and browse options to discover new content.
3. Ask users to search for a radio station or radio show they already listen to, and to see if it is available via **Stitcher**. Use the search bar in the upper right.
4. Or, use the links along the left-side navigation menu to browse shows, listen to live radio, access saved stations, or see friend activity, if you are using this app with social media links.
5. Tap "Browse shows," and have everyone select an interest by which to browse. This is mostly talk radio content. Tap "Live Radio." Then ask users to first see local options available by tapping "Nearby Live Radio," which uses the iPad's GPS and location services. Then participants can browse other programs, including music.
6. Tap "Location" to find content from other countries, or from specific places. This last option is a great way to support foreign-language learning by accessing real, native broadcasts.

Consider adding the app **Spotify** to this program if your users are already Spotify users. It allows users to search for any artist, track, or album by tapping the search icon. Use the Radio icon to create and access music via genre, or to listen to one of the app's recommended stations. Note that this app requires an account, so you should make a dummy account for participants or let users log in with their own credentials. One downside of this app is that it comes with only 48 hours of free trial music playing, which may not last long enough for several programs.

Enhance the literacy enrichment and practice in this program by having the participants write a promotional paragraph that describes their personal radio station. Or, consider pairing this program with **Logo Maker** and having participants create a logo for their radio station.

From *iPads in the Library: Using Tablet Technology to Enhance Programs for All Ages* by Joel A. Nichols.
Santa Barbara, CA: Libraries Unlimited. Copyright © 2013.

SONGSTER

Goals: To experience music-making apps, and to use **GarageBand** to create their own song.

Apps: GarageBand, **Piano**, **CagePianoFree**

Planning Notes: Participants will first use two piano emulators, one traditional and one experimental, and then be walked through a basic tutorial of **GarageBand**, Apple's proprietary and powerful music-creation app. Plan a lot of time for users to tinker with their songs, and consider stretching this program over more than one programming session or by making in part of a series in music programs.

Books/Other Materials: Pots and pans, toy or real instruments, nuts, bolts, screws, nails, files, tin cans, etc., to make unusual sounds.

Instructions:

1. First, open **Piano.** Notice that the piano emulator looks and sounds like a real piano. However, you have to scroll to the sides to see all the keys. If anyone in the group can play the piano, ask them to try it out and share their thoughts. Then ask: Is this like a real piano? How and how not? Does it sound authentic or of high quality? How does it sound different from a real piano?

2. Next, open **CagePianoFree**. This is an experimental music app based on the work of John Cage and his Prepared Piano. This app mirror's Cage's on-stage deconstruction of a piano and manipulation of its strings inside with screws, bolts, nuts, washers, and hooks of various shapes.

3. Participants can tap the hardware items to play notes. Tap the REC icon to begin recording. Play the hardware notes in whatever combination. Then tap the orange stop button.

4. Users can name and save their recordings.

5. Then tap the arrows icon to randomize the hardware and strings available. Let participants play and record many samples and encourage them to press the arrow keys for more notes and hardware several times.

From iPads in the Library: Using Tablet Technology to Enhance Programs for All Ages by Joel A. Nichols.
Santa Barbara, CA: Libraries Unlimited. Copyright © 2013.

Figure 5.2
John Cage's Prepared Piano App simulates this famous augmented piano experiment.

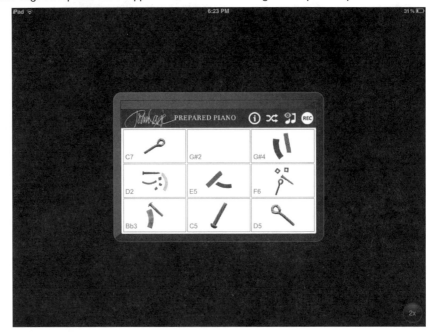

Screenshot courtesy John Cage Trust.

Figure 5.3
Turn the names of the notes in the Prepared Piano App on or off with just one tap.

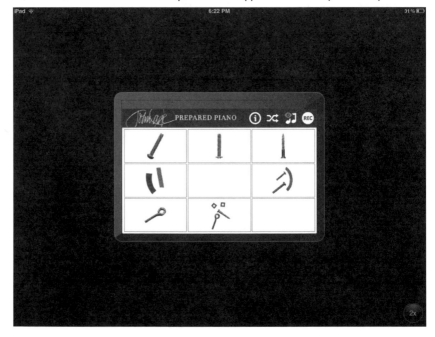

Screenshot courtesy John Cage Trust.

For younger users for whom **GarageBand** is too complicated, or if you do not have access to **GarageBand**, consider continuing this program with these two piano emulators. Ask them to compare the sounds. Or, have pots and pans, plastic sheets, tin cans, nuts, screws, bolts, or washers on hand to make sound. Challenge students to recreate their virtual music with analogue tools.

Now open **GarageBand**. This app has a complex interface and many options beyond the scope of amateurs. Open the project "Curtain-Call Demo," in order to walk users through the basic functionality of the app.

Remind them that most songs, especially the ones they know and love, are made by mixing tracks together in the studio and not played live: vocal tracks, guitars, drums, piano, etc. When "Curtain-Call" loads, users will see pictures of instruments down the left-hand side of the screen. Each instrument has a colored bar—indicating music—for a certain increment to the right. Users can move and alter these recordings by remixing and by changing their locations.

Show users the in-app help by tapping the question mark icon in the upper right. Review what the navigation buttons do. These are:

- The instrument icon
- The mixer icon
- The play and record buttons

In addition, there are the "Apple loops," prerecorded bits of music users can manipulate.

1. Tap "Play." Listen to the song as it plays. Users can follow the vertical bar as it tracks rightward across the screen, showing when each instrument is playing, including the vocals.
2. Tap the vocals icon, and in the new menu, tap "Robot" or "Monster," two of the voice distortion filters that will demonstrate quickly and clearly how changing instrument (in this case, the voice) settings affect the song in the mixer.
3. Move through all of the instruments, selecting different ones or changing the options on the ones already there. Be sure to direct participants to constantly replay the song with the new changes they have made. What effects do they like? What instruments are interesting or compelling to them?
4. As long as they or you like, users should keep experimenting with this demonstration song. When they are reading, they can start their own song project by clicking "My Songs" in the upper left-hand corner and then selecting the plus sign. Tap "New Song."
5. The next menu contains the virtual instruments available to play and record from. Participants can chose from a variety of pianos, keyboard, and drum emulators, or use the "Smart Drums," "Smart Strings," "Smart Bass," "Smart Keyboard," and "Smart Guitar" options for instrument emulators that do not require prior knowledge of any of these instruments. In addition, users can record their own audio from this menu, or record sounds to sample.
6. Select "Smart Strings." Users can filter more specific instrument choices by category first (Cinematic, Modern, Pop, or Romantic), and then pick which instrument to record (first violin, second violin, viola, cello, or upright bass). Participants can also choose to play either chords or notes, and can tap the choice accordingly in the upper right-hand corner of the screen. Chords make it easier for complete music novices to make interesting sounds.

7. Have users practice playing some chords with whichever category and instrument they have chosen. When they are ready to record a track, tap the red record button in the top center of the screen. Play the cords by tapping them. Direct them to use one or multiple fingers.

8. To see the recorded track in the mixer, tap the mixer icon, which is located along the upper navigation bar just to the left of the Play/Record/Rewind buttons. It is next to the instrument control button, which at this point will be shaped like a stringed instrument because of the selection above.

9. Tap the button labeled "Instruments." This will return the instrument selector menu to the screen. Select "Smart Drums."

10. Tap "Hip Hop Drum Machine" to choose from the following options: Hip Hop Drum Machine, Classic Drum Machine, House Drum Machine, Classic Studio Kit, Vintage Kit, and Live Rock Kit. Then drag individual drum pieces into the rhythm space in the middle of the screen. Distribute the individual drum pieces along the four sides of the square area in the middle of the screen—Simple, Loud, Complex, or Quiet—to achieve the perfect drum beat, or tap the dice for a random selection. This is set up with the Loud/Quiet options along the Y axis and Simple/Complex along the X axis.

11. Tap the red button to record. Remember that while you are recording, you can drag the drum pieces around, dragging them up or down the Y axis to make it louder or quieter, along the X axis from simple to complex, or in diagonal lines to combine these effects.

12. Tap the red button to finish recording.

13. Tap the mixer icon to see this track in the mixer.

Participants should keep adding desired tracks until they have all the sound they need to mix together their song. Direct users to remix accordingly and add distortion or other effects. Remind them of the "Curtain-Call Demo" at this point; their own song project should be starting to look a lot like that demo in terms of number and length of tracks.

PHOTO 101

Goal: To teach a variety of photograph and image editing techniques.

Apps: Camera, PS Express, Snapseed, Pixlromatic, Miniatures, Animated GIF, FastCam

Planning Notes: Several of these apps are free. You can easily run this program with whichever free photo apps you are comfortable using. This program could serve as the first in a series of media creation programs for teens. **Snapseed** is a free app that used to be a pay app. It is powerful and easy to use.

Instructions:

The first and most essential app for this program is the built-in camera. Open it. Ask students to take a picture, and then reverse the camera by tapping the icon shaped like a camera with an arrow. Direct participants to take pictures with both the front- and rear-facing cameras.

Show them another camera app, FastCam. This app starts taking pictures the second the app is opened, and takes a steady stream of photos in burst mode. It is great for smartphone users who can never get their camera out of their pocket in time to catch a special moment. Encourage teens to switch back and forth between these cameras as they take photos in the next part of the program.

Give participants 5–10 minutes to take photos inside the library. If your programming space is more limited, consider having photo and art books available so students can experiment with taking photographs of photographs to modify.

Note: consider incorporating any lesson about copyright and fair use. Teach users about Creative Commons licenses and how they can use other people's art in derivative, legal, and ethical ways. For the purposes of this program, though, consider their experimentation in the library as fair use. These projects do not have to be published or shared.

For **PS Express**, tap "Edit," then "Select photo" to import an image from the photo roll. (Like many other image apps, this one also has an in-app camera. Tap the camera icon to access it.)

In this free version, users have limited editing options. These are located behind icons along the bottom of the screen on the left side. The first, the crop tool, has cropping, straightening, rotating, and flipping. The next, light/color levels, has options for exposure, adjustment, color and balance. The next has image transformation options: "Black & White" to turn the image into a black-and-white image, "Colorize" to change the dominant color of the image, "Sketch" for an effect that makes the photo look hand-drawn, "Soft Focus" to blur and cloud the image, "Sharpen" to do the opposite, and "Reduce Noise" to reduce/increase fine detail level.

In all of these cases, users control the effect by sliding their finger along a slider bar. At any time, tap the X to return to the original picture, or use the Undo/Redo buttons. Users can also save or cancel by tapping the buttons in the upper right.

Here are some specific tasks to teach users about these effects.

1. Crop the most interesting section of your photo. Tap the "Crop" tool, then "Crop." A cropping frame will appear. Everything inside the box is highlighted, and the light and color outside the box is grayed out. Move the corners of the crop box with your fingertip until users have the desired size. Or, move the entire box around by dragging from the center. Tap the checkmark in the lower right to crop the image.

2. Next, practice flipping and rotating the photo. Tap "Crop," then "Flip." Tap the object on its side and it will lip over the X axis. To rotate, press down on the edge of the image and rotate in either clock direction without lifting your fingertip.

3. Use the color/light levels icon to explore lightening a very dark picture (tap "Exposure"). To adjust hue and saturation to transform and highlight colors in the picture, tap "Color." Users can control the hue level by moving their finger left and right and the saturation by moving their finger up and down. Point out what happens at either end of the extreme. With no saturation, the image is black and white. With total saturation, adjusting the hue can create very unnatural colors, especially for pets and human skin and hair tones.

4. The most interesting image transformation option to use with participants is **Sketch**. Tap the image transform icon (shaped like a circle with dots inside) and slide your finger up and down to use the sketch effect. Note: This effect will look more hand drawn in black-and-white photos. Ask participants to try it with a color photo. Then use the transform tool's black-and-white option to try the effect again with a black-and-white photo.

Snapseed has a simple help menu to help navigate, and also has links to online videos. Access them by tapping "Help." This app has a series of built-in effects that users can access by scrolling right and left with their fingertips along the bottom of the screen. Each effect tool is controlled by scrolling left or right on the image itself, which moves the level up and down a slider bar. In addition, there are other options that you access by first scrolling your fingertip up and down to select an effect, and then right to left for the level.

1. Tap "Tune Image." Notice that the first effect is "Brightness." Reveal the other effects with an up/down scroll and notice that "Ambiance," "Contrast," "Saturation," and "White Balance" are all available in addition. Practice changing the values for each effect and ask participants to notice what happens.

2. At any point, tap the "Compare" icon at the bottom of the screen to see your progress compared to the original photograph. The other standard tools are "Auto Correct," "Selective Adjust," "Straighten," "Crop," and "Details." Tap "Details."

3. Tap "Loupe," which is along the bottom. This will insert a magnifying window for a particular part of the photo for fine detail work. Scroll up/down to select "Sharpening," and then slide left/right to sharpen or soften the image. Use the loupe tool to work on a specific part of the image. There are several built-in filters that combine the effects accessed above automatically. These are: "Black & White," "Vintage," "Drama," "Grunge," "Center Focus," "Frames" and "Tilt Shift."

4. Tap "Vintage." Use the up/down scroll to select between "Brightness," "Saturation," "Texture Strength," "Center Size," and "Style Strength," and then the left/right scroll to change the values.

5. Tap "Apply," in the lower right-hand corner. Then users can select to "Compare" to the original, "Revert" for earlier versions, "Save" to save it in the Photo Roll, or "Share" to export via

email, Flickr, Facebook, or Twitter or by printing. Note that increasing "Texture Strength" to the maximum makes the effect very easy to see and demonstrate. Because this app is so powerful, some of the finer adjustments can be hard for beginners to see and understand. Another option in this tool that shows similar dramatic effect is setting the "Center Size" to zero.

6. The last option to explore explicitly with users is "Tilt-Shift." This option changes the focus on some parts of the photo and increases the distance between the objects and the background. The effect highlights a part of a photo, and makes real objects look like miniatures or models. Tap "Tilt Shift." Two sets of parallel lines appear over your photo with a blue dot in between them. Move the blue dot to the section of the image you want to be most in focus. The spaces demarked by the sets of parallel lines allow the user to control how much of the photo is in focus. Pinch open and close it to increase and decrease the space between these lines. This effect is most dramatic on an image with a lot going on in different planes. The ideal is long views with action in the foreground and at least two layers of background. Have good samples for students to work on, or consider allowing them to shoot some images from an upper-story window or other good vantage point.

Next, demonstrate a simple animation technique with **Loopcam**. This app makes animated GIFs, short animated loops of still pictures. Loopcam allows users to take up to 50 still pictures.

Along the bottom, click settings to manage social media connections. This app requires a login either to Twitter, Facebook, or Tumblr in order to share or save these animated GIFs.

Along the top of the screen, there are three icons. The first is a ghost, which superimposes a transparent image of the last photo taken over the camera input so users can line up their still animation more precisely. The middle icon is a camera flash. The icon on the right changes the camera feed from the front camera to the back.

1. Open **Loopcam**. Tap the camera icon to take the first picture. A "1" will appear in the counter to the left of the camera icon. Direct participants to take as many photos as they want. Encourage them to make a serious face, then a very goofy face, or a very dramatically different face or pose. This makes a good quick demonstration project.
2. Tap the arrow so the loop will compile and playback.
3. Then tap "Done" to share it via one of the social media services.

VIDEO 101

Goal: For teens to capture video and learn basic video editing techniques

Apps: Camera, Splice, iMovie

Planning Notes: This program works well with participants in groups of two or three sharing one device.

Books/Other Materials: Toy fans, pinwheels, tops, wind-up toys, rubber balls, etc.

Instructions:
Pass out the toys. Ask participants to familiarize themselves with how their toys move, and then set up a filming area on their table. They should aim the iPad camera in such a way that they can capture the motion of the object without having to move the camera.

Using **Camera**, take up to 10 practice shoots of the object in motion. Make sure there is enough light for a clear image. Shoot several more images.

1. In **Splice**, tap the plus sign to create a new project, and name the project. The following screen allows participants to choose basic settings for HD/SD, Border, Orientation, and Default transition. Leave these settings at their defaults and tap "Done."
2. Tap the central frame of the blank project space to import new video clips, photos, or transitions. Tap anything from the Photo Roll and select it for import. At this point in the import, participants will be asked whether they want to add default transitions or not. Tell them to choose no.
3. Tap the first clip on the pencil icon, to edit. This isolates a given clip, and allows additional editing. The blue icons along the bottom allow users to, in order:
   * Trim the messy ends/false starts from a given clip (scissors)
   * Change the speed of the video playback (running figure)
   * Crop tool
   * Duplicate the clip (x2)
   * Delete the clip (trash can).
4. Shoot the object in action. Shoot take after take, until there are at least 30 to 60 seconds of video total. Alter your footage by speeding up and slowing down the footage. Try speeding it up in one part of the video, and slowing it down in others.
5. Challenge participants to use the speed, trimming, and crop tools to distort the action in some way. Tap "Preview," and then "Export." Chose medium for faster processing and smaller files for sharing.

In **iMovie**, you will also import video clips (or stills) and then manipulate them. Follow the onscreen instructions to import clips. In this program, participants will record directly into **iMovie**. Tap the videocamera icon. This app displays a three-screen editing deck. The upper half of the screen shows, on the right side, the video you are editing. On the left are individual clips available to add to the project. (Note that these are shown in a frame-by-frame view).

From *iPads in the Library: Using Tablet Technology to Enhance Programs for All Ages* by Joel A. Nichols.
Santa Barbara, CA: Libraries Unlimited. Copyright © 2013.

1. To add photos or music, click the icons along the bottom of this subwindow.
2. To add them to the project, double-tap on any clip, and the clip will sweep down into the editing space on the lower half of the screen.
3. Manipulate the footage in the bottom half of the screen with your fingertips. Double-tap to insert titles and control their styles. Tap clips to highlight them in yellow, and then drag the yellow edge forward or back to extend or shorten a clip.
4. Shoot the object in action. Shoot take after take, until there are at least 30–60 seconds of video total.
5. Import as many clips as you like into the project window.
6. As in **Splice**, mentioned previously, challenge user to distort the action of their object with the video tools. Click the settings icon on the upper right. The top row of options show color schemes and motifs, including a CNN-style news crawl template.
7. Participants should also experiment with adding theme music, fading frames in or out, and trimming the clips. Direct them to rotate the images, by grasping with two fingers on the frame in the viewer window and turning them clockwise or counterclockwise.

Allow plenty of supervised time—at least 20 minutes—for participants to experiment with their movement distortions before they save their work and share their work.

VIDEO SURVEY

Goals: To practice basic video editing skills, including integrating still visuals into a video, and to make a survey with both qualitative and quantitative questions.

Apps: Camera, Splice, iMovie, Pages or Keynote

Planning Notes: Splice is an iPhone app that you must use at reduced resolution on an iPad; but it is free and highly functional.

Instructions:

In this program, participants will make a short video that documents a survey question. This survey will have two questions.

The first question is quantitative, which means you will measure it with numbers. For example: How many times did you eat fresh fruit this week? How many Facebook likes did you leave on friends' pages? What is your favorite day of the week?

The second question is qualitative, so it will measure individual responses. For example: What kinds of fresh fruit did you eat this week? What kinds of things do "like" when you see them on Facebook? Why do you prefer Fridays over Saturdays?

Prompt participants to draft two questions about the same topic, one quantitative and one qualitative. Then each participant should ask everyone in the room their quantitative question and tally the answer.

1. Open **Pages**. Open a new document by tapping the plus sign in the upper left corner. Then tap the insert button, and also the plus sign icon, on the upper right of the document menu. Choose charts, and then pick one of the options in either 2D and 3D. There are options for bar graphs, pie charts, and line graphs.
2. Once the chosen chart template is inserted into the document, tap on it and then choose the "edit data" button that pops up. The chart simply counts the number of responses for each choice. For example, three people said they ate fresh fruit twice last week, five people said they ate fresh fruit four times last week, and one person said he or she did not eat any. So the chart has three data points: 3, 2; 5, 4; 1, 0. Or: six participants said that Friday was their favorite day of the week; two said that Saturday was their favorite; and one said that Wednesday was their favorite. This chart has the following three data points: 6, Friday; 2, Saturday; 1, Wednesday.
3. Have participants take a screenshot of this graph, to store it on the photo roll for later use.
4. Next, participants will ask each other the qualitative question, and film at least three responses: What kinds of fruit did you eat, why do you prefer Saturdays?
5. Open **Camera**. In the lower right, move the slider from the camera icon to the video camera icon. Ask participants to check the light and picture quality, and to map out a "set." If they are using an iPad stand (or a library-constructed one, out of duct tape and bookends), will they ask each interviewee to sit in a particular chair? Will they hold the iPad up to capture someone's face? Do they want a handheld/shaky documentary look, or a more stable "studio" look? Do they want to use the rear-facing camera or to include themselves, the interviewer, with the forward camera? Will they be shooting in portrait or landscape mode?

From *iPads in the Library: Using Tablet Technology to Enhance Programs for All Ages* by Joel A. Nichols.
Santa Barbara, CA: Libraries Unlimited. Copyright © 2013.

6. When everyone has picked where and how they will shoot their footage, participants will start interviewing and recording responses.
7. Tap the round red record button on the right-hand side of the screen to begin recording. The red button will blink, and a timer showing elapsed recorded time will appear in the upper right. Film as many responses as time allows. Remind everyone to keep their answers to 10 or 15 seconds.

Use **Splice** or **iMovie**. In **Splice**, tap the plus sign to create a new project, and name the project. The following screen allows participants to choose basic settings.

- HD/SD: high definition or standard definition, which refer here to different aspect rations.
- Border: to add a decorative border (or not) around the video
- Orientation: participants should pick landscape or portrait based on how they have decide to film their subjects.
- Default transition: five basic transition effects to choose from.

Then tap "Done."

1. Tap the central frame of the blank project space to import new video clips, photos, or transitions. Remember that the chart is going to be one still photo we insert, but that participants can also insert a title card.
2. Chose the selected image from the Photo Roll and select it for import.
3. At this point in the import, participants can choose to add default transitions or not. The project space will display each imported clip and, in between them, gray blocks representing transitions.
4. Tap the first clip on the pencil icon, to edit. This isolates a given clip, and allows additional modification. The blue icons along the bottom allow users to, in order:
   - Trim the messy ends/false starts from a given clip (scissors)
   - Change the speed of the video playback (running figure)
   - Crop tool
   - Duplicate the clip (x2)
   - Delete the clip (trash can)
5. Make any needed adjustments to the clip. The most common ones for this video survey will probably be trimming ends, cropping, and deleting.
6. Adjust each clip and each transition as needed, by tapping the pencil icon to edit.
7. At any point, you can tap on one of the plus signs to add another clip.
8. Remind participants to import their graphs. At this point, they could also make title cards in **Pages**. A title card might state the question and their name, or they could be more elaborate. Teens will then need to import their title cards, as they did with the graphs.
9. To add music or sound, tap the audio icon. The display will change and show a frame-by-frame ribbon of the edited video at the top. Under that, there are three audio tracks. The first two, marked by a musical note, allow users to import tracks from iTunes or from a selection of built-in sound effects. The third music track is marked by a microphone icon, and allows users to offer voice-over.
10. Once voice-over or sound effects are added to these tracks, they appear as orange-colored blocks that can be moved and adjusted. Tap and drag them to move the snippets around the audio track. Tap and release to control fade or to trim the edges.

11. When participants are finished adding audio to their edited clip, tap "Preview." Direct them to play the clip all the way through, and if they are happy, click "Export." Chose high or medium. (Medium will be a smaller file and will also render more quickly.) When the file renders, it will automatically be copied to the photo roll.

In **iMovie**, tap the plus sign for a new project. In this app, you will also import video clips (or stills) and then manipulate them. Follow the onscreen instructions to import clips. (You can also record directly into **iMovie**: tap the video camera icon or, for voice-over, the microphone).

This app displays a three-screen editing deck. The upper half of the screen shows, on the right side, the video you are editing. On the left are individual clips available to add to the project. (Note that these are shown in a frame-by-frame view.) To add photos or music, click the icons along the bottom of this subwindow.

To add them to the project, double-tap on any clip, and the clip will sweep down into the editing space on the lower half of the screen.

Manipulate the footage in the bottom half of the screen with your fingertips. Double-tap to insert titles and control their styles. Tap clips to highlight them in yellow, and then drag the yellow edge forward or back to extend or shorten a clip.

When the movie project is done, tap the document with a star to return to the front page of the app. From there, tap the right-pointing arrow icon to save to the Photo Roll, or export to YouTube or Facebook.

NOW IN THEATERS!

Goal: To create a movie trailer for an imaginary blockbuster movie. Participants will plan a mood, story idea, and characters, and then create a short movie trailer video. This program works best with participants working in groups of 2–5.

Apps: Camera, iMovie, YouTube

Planning Notes: Ahead of time, find at least two movie trailers to show. Pick upcoming movies that are of high interest to your audience.

Instructions:
Show the teens your sample trailers. Then ask them to search YouTube for the trailer of an upcoming movie. They should watch it a few times, and then let them know that they will be making a trailer of their own.

1. Open **iMovie**. Tap the plus sign along the bottom of the screen. Tap "New Trailer" from the pop-up. This app has several built-in trailer styles users should choose from. Scroll to the right along the bottom to see and preview these styles. The available templates range from Bollywood to retro, scary to superhero.
2. Users can tap the style they want to preview. A sample trailer will play, showing various options available in the template. Once users have picked a style, direct them to tap "Create," the blue button in the upper right.
3. Fill in the credits as desired by tapping on one of the lines. The keyboard will appear. Tap the Storyboard tab and walk users through the template shot by shot. For example, in the "scary" template, users will have preset title cards that tell a typical scary movie structure. Blank shots with gray template figures show users what kind of scene to film to plug into the template. Users can customize the title cards by tapping on them and changing the text.
4. In the upper right quadrant, tap "Play" on the video. This is the video users will create, swapping in their own video for the one with gray figures.
5. Have users record their videos by using the Camera application in **iMovie**. When they have sufficient footage or perhaps a minute or more, they should return to the trailer they were working on. The video clips will appear in the lower right quadrant of the screen.
6. To import some of these clips into the trailer, first select the gray template box. Then tap the desired clip where you want to start, and a yellow selector will appear. Drag it to the right with your finger until all the desired footage is selected. Then tap the blue arrow to send the selected footage into the appropriate part of the template.
7. Direct users to play the video periodically to reorient themselves and check their work along the way. *Hint*: the right-hand play icon plays a preview; the left-hand play icon loads the trailer in full-screen mode.
8. When users are satisfied with their trailer, have them tap the icon shaped like a document with a star on it. This returns users to the home screen.

Direct users to come together and show the whole class their trailers. Users can then tap the share icon (an arrow coming out of a box) to save this trailer to the camera roll, export it to YouTube or share it on Facebook or on other social media services.

From *iPads in the Library: Using Tablet Technology to Enhance Programs for All Ages* by Joel A. Nichols. Santa Barbara, CA: Libraries Unlimited. Copyright © 2013.

TIME LAPSE GERMINATION

Goal: To learn basic plant physiology by making a time lapse video of seeds germinating.

Apps: StoMo, iBloom, YouTube (or other video content delivered via **Safari**)

Planning Notes: Schedule this program over several days. This gives participants an opportunity to capture a variety of still images over the germination period, which will take at least five to seven days and possibly as long as two weeks. For this reason, the program works best in a classroom setting where participants can access the experiment frequently. It can work in a library setting, but I recommend that the librarian capture several additional images a day even if the participants are not there.

Books/Other Materials: Seeds that germinate quickly, such as beans, radish, lettuce, dianthus, or marigold.

Instructions:
Begin this program by defining the process of germination and explaining that seeds need a few things to become plants, especially water and heat.

Show a diagram from the Web or from a book with the basic plant parts. Explain that the food a plant needs to start growing is already inside the seed. Water and heat tell the seed it is time to do its work.

Consider germinating seeds on damp paper towels or paper plates rather than in soil. Of course a seed can grow in soil, but you would capture only the germination action on film that happens once the seedlings sprout above the soil. Without soil, it is easier to see the seed split and the plant matter to begin differentiating into roots and shoots.

Show a time lapse video or animation of seeds sprouting to demonstrate the kind of film participants will ultimately be making. Explain that these videos take pictures at regular intervals, say once an hour (or once a minute or day) over long periods of time and then put them together to show the action. Or that video is shot over very long periods of time continuously and then played back at a faster rate.

1. Open **StoMo**. This app allows participants to capture images and keep track of them in the right-hand project window. Participants can choose the front camera or the rear one, and they can set the "frame match" and "frames per second" slider bar to the appropriate levels. For this program, they set the "frame match" rate to the middle of the slider bar. This will keep a transparent image of the last frame captured over the camera display window and make it easier to line up the camera.

   It is critical that the camera is in the same position for each frame and remains in the same position for all the images captured. To this end, mark out a space to serve as the set, marking the fixed positions of the camera and the plate or tray on which the seeds are germinating.

From *iPads in the Library: Using Tablet Technology to Enhance Programs for All Ages* by Joel A. Nichols.
Santa Barbara, CA: Libraries Unlimited. Copyright © 2013.

2. Tap the "Capture" button to set capture mode, and then tap "Capture Image" at the bottom of the right-hand column. Encourage them to take many shots each day, at each step of the process. The more frames captured, both the longer and smoother the result.

3. Set the "Frames Per Second" slider bar in playback mode to modify how quickly or slowly the images animate and play as video. Remind participants that the fastest animation option in this app is 30 frames per second, so for every second in length they want their final product to be, they will need at least 30 frames.

4. On days one and two, recording 30 or 50 frames is likely enough. However, as the seeds start to sprout, the more often you capture images, the better your final product will be. This could mean that you, as the adult supervisor, takes some pictures first thing in the morning, then again around midday, with the afterschool crowd when they come in, and then perhaps even again at the very end of the day. If participants are to take all of the frames themselves, have them do at least 50 at the beginning of the program time, and 50 at the end, even if it is only an hour later.

5. After every capture, participants should tap the Playback option and then press the "Play" button at the bottom of the video window to check their progress. Remind them to experiment with the rate of "Frames per Second" by adjusting the slider bar.

6. Repeat this over a series of days, until the seeds have become sprouts.

7. By the end of two weeks, participants will have hundreds of captured frames to compile into a time-lapse video. Use the project window on the right-hand side to select individual frames to delete (in case there were any capture errors or stray fingers in front of the camera).

8. Make final adjustments to the "Frames per Second" rate until participants are happy with the final product. Then tap the "Export to Library" button, in the center under the video screen, and the video will play as it exports. **StoMo** will pop up a message reading "successfully saved the video to your library. The video can be found in the 'Photos' app," which you can clear by tapping 'OK.' "

9. Post your results on a Library or classroom YouTube channel or social media feed, or send it via email.

Here is a program variation that targets similar scientific literacy goals without actually conducting the germination experiment. Instead of germinating seeds over a period of days, use the app **iBloom**, which simulates a plant growing. This is an iPhone-optimized app, so you will have to use it magnified and with resolution loss or on a smaller screen.

1. Tap "Start." Pick "Standard Flowers" or "Seasonal Flowers." Encourage participants to pick different flowers. (First-time users can tap "Tutorial" first for a quick and interactive overview of the options detailed below.) Note that in Standard Flowers, there is only one free option. In season, there are five free options and more to purchase.

2. Water your flower by tapping the water icon and tilting the device to the side, as you would a watering can. There is a water sound effect and animation. Provide airflow to your seed or plant by tapping the air icon. If you blow into the microphone or by swiping one finger up the screen, you will hear a wind effect and see animation. Finally, feed your plant by tapping the food icon and shaking the device to spread the plant food. You will also notice sound and animation effects.

3. There are two play modes. Classic mode uses real-time growth time to grow the flowers. This is only practical if you are running this program over a long period of time. Select

instead accelerated mode to grow a plant in just a few minutes. The icons will change color to yellow and to red if the plant is lacking in air, water, or food.

Encourage participants to vary the amounts of water, air, and food to see the effect on the growth process. Ask participants to share any observations about this digital experiment: What happens if plants get too much water and not enough food or air, for example? If no one experiences this problem, instruct them to rerun their digital experiment and to withhold air and food from a healthy sprout. Is this how real-life plants would behave?

ACTION FIGURE PARTY

Goal: To make a stop-motion animated video clip. Participants will choose some objects to serve as actors, work out a storyline, and then film a stop motion clip.

Apps: iMotion HD, **YouTube App** (or YouTube content delivered by Safari), **Vimeo**

Planning Notes: Ahead of time, make a sample stop-motion video. Follow the directions below. Very simple ones to make in 10 minutes or less include: a piece of fruit or vegetable that crawls or roll across a table; a book opening and fluttering its own pages, or a bowl of marbles that vanish one by one and then reappear. Creating a sample clip not only provides you with a sample you can show participants, but also will make troubleshooting participants' clips easier.

Consider showing examples from **YouTube** or **Vimeo**.

Note that if you do not already have a cover or stand for your iPad, or you will want to make one. Make an excellent and simple stand using duct tape and a large metal bookend that will keep the iPad camera pointed at the right angle. Be sure to avoid the camera when affixing the tape.

Books/Other Materials: Poseable action figures, dolls, or other toys and objects; clay; other household objects or office supplies (fruit/vegetables, paper clips, etc.).

Instructions:

At the beginning of the program, show participants your sample movie, as well as some more elaborate stop-motion animations. Use the **YouTube** app (or **Safari**) to show samples you have picked out earlier. You can also use examples from inside the app, accessible via tapping the "iMotion gallery" button.

Help participants pick out objects they can use to tell a story. Again, inching a piece of fruit across the table is great for a beginner. More elaborate stories and animations are possible using highly pose-able objects such as action figures. Action figures or toys from a popular or well-known franchise have the added benefit of appealing to reluctant participants. Clay is very easy to work with, but participants are then limited by their own artistic ability to fashion figures.

Direct participants to map out about 30 seconds of action for their objects. They should consider the usual and unusual ways they can animate the object: What is the object's natural behavior? If they have picked an orange: should it peel itself, should it juice itself, or could it eat itself? Or, should this orange behave more like a car or truck, stand in for a soccer ball, etc.

Here are some library-focused ideas to try out:

- A shelf of books that rearranges itself. Perhaps the books rearrange themselves in alphabetical order, or in call number order. Consider having them first arrange themselves in size or color order before deciding to go a more traditional route.
- Read or tell an age-appropriate folktale or story, and then ask participants to retell some part of the story in their clip. Even with teens, consider using a highly visual and conceptual picture

From *iPads in the Library: Using Tablet Technology to Enhance Programs for All Ages* by Joel A. Nichols.
Santa Barbara, CA: Libraries Unlimited. Copyright © 2013.

book such as *Little Blue and Little Yellow* by Leo Leonni or *Press Here* by Hervé Tullet. These books would serve as powerful inspiration for claymation clips.

Mark the space for the set, and rehearse how the objects are going to move.

Using **iMotion HD**, tap "New Movie" to access the screen to set up your clip. Fill in a title in that field. This app allows remote access for time-lapse photography. Ignore the options "Time-lapse" and "Remoted" for now. Tap "Manual" and then "Start." While this app can capture sound with the microphone, the program works better filming silent clips and then setting them to music later.

Mark on the table with tape where the iPad will be positioned during filming. As you move the objects and tap the screen, it might move out of place. For the smoothest animation, the camera should stay as still as possible.

Use the "Options" button to select "Grid" and "Onion Skin." Grid superimposes green directional lines over the image on the display for precise line-up. "Onion Skin" ghosts the previous image in over the display—overlaying the last frame transparently—so users can control the exact amount of movement per frame.

You can, in postproduction, select how long each frame will appear, from 1 frame per second to 30 frames per second. That means that 30 seconds of very slow action will be at least 30 frames. Practically speaking, participants will need hundreds of frames to make 10–30 seconds of smooth, fast animation. Participants should experiment with different frames per second rates until they have the desired animation effect.

Start filming!

1. Tap "Capture." Slightly move the object.
2. Tap "Capture" again. Repeat. Be forewarned, this process is laborious. Encourage participants who are frustrated with how cool and seamless it will look when they have successfully animated several seconds of animated footage.

     Do not worry about frames that capture a stray hand or finger, or that are errors. Users can delete individual frames in postproduction.
3. When all the frames have been captured, tap "Stop." Note: If and when desired, you can still return to capture more frames.
4. Use the slider bar to set the desired rate of frames per second. The lower the rate, the slower the animation.
5. Use the "Tools" menu to advance frame by frame, if desired. This is the place to delete individual frames. Use the pause button to freeze a frame, and then tap the delete icon on the far right.
6. To resume capturing frames, return to the home screen. Tap "My Movies," and then tap "Resume" on the movie you want to edit.
7. Or, tap "Export" to export this film to your iPad's photo library or to Facebook. From the photo library, you can play it on other devices, use in other apps, email, or post to social media.

Encourage participants to find some way to take their movie with them—by posting it to their own pages or by emailing it to themselves, and by showing it to the other participants at the end of the program.

DESIGN WORKSHOP

Figure 5.4
The **Design Museum** app shows each of its object on a detailed page like this one, with information about the object's origin and construction.

Screenshot courtesy Design Museum

Goals: To expose teen participants to the Design Museum of London's collection and to give teens the opportunity to practice building a 3D model with digital and (optional) physical tools.

Apps: Design Museum, 123DSCULPT, Kid Blocks

Books/Other Materials: Clay, building blocks such as Legos.

Instructions:

1. Open **Design Museum**. It displays design objects in a liquid grid that moves in both rows and columns, as users swipe the screen. Demonstrate how this works, and then ask users to sort the objects by categories, using the filters "Architecture," "Furniture," "Graphics," "Products" and "Transportation."
2. Ask users to spend five minutes browsing. Direct users to use the heart icon to mark certain objects as favorites to which they will return later. Be sure everyone has selected at least

some objects from the furniture category. Selecting objects brings up short articles. When a participant selects an object, it brings up a short article and an accompanying video from the London museum staff. Tap on the picture for more images. To return to the object page, tap the orange "X" in the upper left. Return to the main grid of exhibited objects by clicking on the plus sign in the upper left, and then the grid icon.

3. Direct participants to pick out a few objects. Ask them which one they find most beautiful. Which are the most useful? Which would they most like to own? Why? Which do they find "ingenious," and why? Moderate a discussion using real examples everyone can look at. Focus in on the furniture categories. What are the objects made of? How were they constructed? What is their purpose? What is their color or shape?

4. Now, tell users that they are going to remake one of these objects using a 3D modeling tool. Open **123Dsculpt**. Users will see options for "Creatures," "Geometry," and "Objects." The preset options are limited, so most participants will find one of the geometric shapes a useful starting point.

5. Treat this shape like a lump of physical clay. Pinch to zoom in and out, and use a one-finger swipe to move the object in space.

6. Reshape the clay by brushing or rubbing your fingertips over it, and use the options located on the left-side icon ribbon to smooth, sharpen, flatten, inflate, move, and deform parts of the clay, as well as apply color and texture. Use the arrows along the top menu to undo mistakes, and tap the camera icon to take screenshots.

7. Remind participants that they will have time to come back to this app in a few minutes, but that you want to show them another 3D modeling tool.

Next, open **KidBlocks**. Demonstrate how to place blocks on the 3D grid.

1. First, tap the green single block. A menu pops up where you can select block size/style, and also shape.

2. Select the style and shape you want, and then tap again on the grid. Tap anywhere on the grid, and a block will appear. Tap it again to make the grid go away. Begin building the desired shape by placing blocks next to each other and on top of each other.

3. Offer participants the opportunity to continue building their object, and challenge them to modify and customize it. Ask them if they will they improve on this object's design, function, form, shape, color, etc., and make it better for their own use. Take screenshots to email, print, or post as a takeaway from this program.

Also, let participants experiment with play dough or clay and/or real blocks if available. This is a great way to adapt the program if there are many more participants than there are iPads.

APP CONCEPT DESIGN

Goals: To design criteria for an app, and then to mock up interactive screens of how the app would work.

Apps: Keynote (to mock up the app), **Design Museum App**, **Qwiki**, **CagePianoFree**, **Lego Self-Portrait**, **PollutionApp**, **Epicurious** (as examples of app design); **Storyboard**, **Pages**, or other word processing app if users prefer to draft electronically rather than on paper (optional).

Planning Notes: This program can be easily adapted as a website design and mockup program.

Books/Other Materials: Scratch paper and pens/pencils to map out the app concept.

Instructions:
Begin the program by asking participants if they have any favorite apps. Ask them to describe what the app does.

Demonstrate several apps. The ones described below are all excellent examples of the different kinds of design, function, and content offered by iPad apps. Feel free to add in other apps as well. Tell participants that you want them to evaluate the following apps based on:

1. Visual design of the interface
2. Interactivity and how the interface works
3. Content delivery or creation (any text, video, photos, audio, etc.)

If possible, make three columns on a chalkboard or large pad of paper to keep track of their observations: FORM, FUNCTION, and CONTENT. Ask users to think about the good and bad aspects of these apps in terms of these three categories.

1. Open **Design Museum App**. Demonstrate how to scroll each column and row left and right and up and down. Encourage users to select specific objects by tapping on them, and to sort via the available filters—"Architecture," "Furniture," "Graphics," "Product," or "Transport"—by tapping on the funnel icon.
2. Open **Qwiki**. Ask users to search for any destination, perhaps somewhere they would like to visit. What do they find? What kind of media and content do they see? Tap "Back" to return to the home screen. Swipe to the left to scroll through categories: "News," "Location," "Popular," "Actors," "Cities," "Natural Wonders," and "Monuments." Ask users to describe what is good about this content. What do users like or dislike about the organization, appearance, or color scheme?
3. Open **CagePianoFree**. This simple app is based on John Cage's experimental Prepared Piano, a partially deconstructed piano manipulated with common hardware, such as nuts, bolts, and screws. Show users how to record and play back music by tapping REC and then tapping the hardware in individual squares. Each bit of hardware on a square corresponds to

piano notes. Tap the arrows icon to load more available notes. Ask users to describe: What do users like about this design? What about the rather spare visuals? Functionally, what does it do? How would you share and export your recordings?

4. Open **Lego Self-Portrait**. This app's sole function is to apply a mosaic photo filter to any photo taken with the in-app camera or imported. In this case, the mosaic is a Lego effect. The only real options are to change the colors of the blocks in the mosaic. This is a great example of a simple and straightforward app that has limited and specific function.

5. Open **PollutionApp.** This app uses your current location within a 30 km radius to show possible sources of air, water, ground, and radio-wave pollution. It integrates a map of these locations with additional data about each company.

6. Open **Epicurious**. Ask users to search for a recipe for their favorite dish using the search box. Explore the ways to browse recipes in this app, the use of visuals, and so on. Can participants think of any ways to improve the delivery of these recipes?

7. Now ask users now to draft design criteria for an app of their own. If they want, they can propose remaking an app they think needs improvement. What kind of app will it be? First, what content does the app contain and deliver? Is it text, pictures, video, audio, or something else?

8. Second, what function does the app perform? Does it use the camera, microphones, accelerometer, GPS, or other hardware to perform this function? If it uses data (such as weather, time, bus schedules, restaurant locations, etc.), where does it get the data? Third, what does the interface look like? How does a user navigate the menus? What colors and images are dominant?

9. Users should draw up to five screens that demonstrate how their app works. Follow the example below, which is a simple, three-screen, interactive mockup of a sample app called "Next Bus!" The function of the sample app is simply to tell library users what time the next buses leave from the stop closest to the library. In this location, two bus lines serve the library, a north-south route (Route 64) and an east-west route (Route 34).

    This app's data would be fed via an API, or application programming interface, to a dataset from a local transit authority. The app also relies on the iPad's built-in clock to know the time.

10. Open **Keynote**. A presentation called "Getting Started" will appear as an option on the screen. This is an app tutorial—in presentation format—that users should review. It contains very specific help and a preview of Keynote's most powerful features. Tap the plus sign to create a new presentation, and then tap "New Slide" in the left-hand slide navigation column to add a new slide. Tap text boxes to edit them.

    For this sample, you will create three slides.

Slide 1
Text/graphic that reads "Next Bus."
Text/graphic/button that reads "Next Route 64."
Text/graphic/button that reads "Next Route 34."
Text/graphic/button that reads "Home."

Slide 2
Text/graphic that says "The next northbound bus leaves at."
Graphic/text box that reads "3:42 PM."
Text/graphic that says "The next southbound bus leaves at."
Graphic/text box that reads "3:54 PM."
Text/graphic/button that reads "Home."

Slide 3

Text/graphic that says "The next eastbound bus leaves at."
Graphic/text box that reads "4:02 PM."
Text/graphic that says "The next westbound bus leaves at."
Graphic/text box that reads "4:06 PM."
Text/graphic/button that reads "Home."

11. The text/graphic/button options are where your design aesthetic comes in. Choose a background from the templates when you create a new presentation; and then add text boxes, photos, or other images as well as charts or shapes. Any of the objects or shapes can have text added to them.

12. Click the plus sign icon on the upper right-hand section to insert new media, tables, charts, or shapes.

13. To enhance the design with animations, select any object, photo, text box, or shape, and then tap "Animate." Select the desired animation effect, and then tap anywhere outside of the menu.

14. You can also enhance the design and interface with transitions between slides. Tap the wrench icon in the upper right-hand corner, and then select "Transitions and Builds." Then select any slide, and tap the plus sign that appears next to it. Next, choose a transition effect in the same way you chose an animation effect, then tap anywhere outside the menu.

15. To make the slides interactive, add hyperlinks to your slides exactly as below. Tap the wrench icon, select "Advanced," then tap "Interactive Hyperlinks." Tap any object and then chose the option "Link to Slide" and pick the appropriate slide number.

Slide 1

Text/graphic that reads "Next Bus."
Text/graphic/button that reads *"Next Route 64."* → hyperlink this object to slide 2.
Text/graphic/button that reads *"Next Route 34."* → hyperlink this object to slide 3.

Slide 2

Text/graphic that says "The next northbound bus leaves at."
Graphic/text box that reads "3:42 PM."
Text/graphic that says "The next southbound bus leaves at."
Graphic/text box that reads "3:54 PM."
Text/graphic/button that reads *"Home."* → hyperlink this object to slide 1.

Slide 3

Text/graphic that says "The next eastbound bus leaves at."
Graphic/text box that reads "4:02 PM."
Text/graphic that says "The next westbound bus leaves at."
Graphic/text box that reads "4:06 PM."
Text/graphic/button that reads *"Home."* → hyperlink this object to slide 1.

This rudimentary interactive mockup simply displays sample bus times and takes users back to the home screen. Users could make more complicated design choices by incorporating with links to maps, or by adding additional bus routes or stops. Show users a sample so the hyperlinking technique is clear. Obviously, in the app criteria, the time of the next bus would be refreshed from the transit authority data for whatever time of day it is.

Users can spend as long as they need to creating appropriate objects and hyperlinking them to simulate interactivity. Consider breaking this program into a series if there is not enough time to finish in one session.

LOGO MAKER

Goal: For users to create a personal logo, or perhaps one for a company, website, project, or band, based on examination and research of corporate and other popular logos.

Apps: LogoCheater, Camera, iWaterFree, PS Express or Snapseed or Fingersketch Pro

Books/Other Materials: Paper, pencils, crayons, markers, other art supplies

Instructions:
Define trademark and copyright for participants, noting that the key difference is that copyright refers to the rights to reproduce or sell content, and that trademark covers the right to use a defined picture, color, word or wording, logo, etc., to promote and sell any particular brand or product. The images in this program would be covered by trademark. Remind users of the limitations in using anyone's trademark for anything other than practice and experimentation.

Make a list, or draw pictures on a chalkboard or large pad of paper, of all the logos participants know of. Encourage any users to come to the chalkboard/pad of paper to draw the logos they suggest.

1. Open **LogoCheater**. This app shows many familiar corporate logos down the left side of the screen. Ask users how many they can identify, and go through the list as a group. Tap "Reveal" on the right-hand side to show the answers.
2. Be sure to point out how some companies use letters or initials in their logo: Amazon's A, Barbie's B, Calvin Klein's CK, McDonald's and MTV's M, for example. Focus in on MTV and McDonald's specifically. They both have logos based on an M, but how are they different? Are they the same shaped M? How do they differentiate from each other in terms of color or shape? Why do you think the corporate designers of these two logos made the choices they did? How does each logo effectively telegraph what the brand is "selling" to the consumer without explicitly showing products or services?
3. Next, tap "Menu," and then change the **LogoCheater** to level 9. These logos will be much more obscure and less recognizable. Does any participant recognize any of them? Explore and tap "Reveal," noting if there are any companies or logos that participants do recognize. Pick some examples and ask dissecting questions about the image or shape of the logo, the object pictured if applicable, and the colors or other designs used. Encourage users to explore all nine levels, and to isolate up to three logos they consider their favorites.
4. Direct users to redraw these logos using paper and art supplies. In their drawings, they should highlight what they like the most about the logo. Ask the teens to come back together and share what logo they picked, why they picked it, and what they like the best about it.
5. Next, have users create their own logo. Ask them to make up a new logo for an existing company or product. Users can also make their own personal logo to use on their Facebook page or other web presence.

From *iPads in the Library: Using Tablet Technology to Enhance Programs for All Ages* by Joel A. Nichols.
Santa Barbara, CA: Libraries Unlimited. Copyright © 2013.

6. Direct participants to sketch out their new logo using paper and pencil so they have an example to work from when they start sketching digitally.

Once they have a sketch, they have many options for proceeding. First, users can use an existing image they find online to edit and manipulate; second, users could use the Camera to take a photograph of their paper sketch, and then continue to edit it digitally; or third, users could use an application such as **FingerSketch** to draw an image based on their design. If using **Snapseed** or **PS Express**, refer to the instructions in the Photo 101 program.

1. To use **FingerSketch**, open it. Tap the first option, Finger Sketch Paint. This app's interface is more or a less a blank screen with just a few options at the top. From the dropdown menu, chose between line styles. The styles range from simple lines (Sketchy) to lines with shading or textures, including "Fur," "Longfur," "Web" (as in spider web), "Squares," "Paint" or "Ribbon." The final option, "Eraser," allows users to erase any lines they have created. Direct users to select one of these line styles.

2. As users draw with their fingertips, they will notice that the line style becomes more pronounced with more pressure or thicker lines. Give them several minutes to experiment using the side of their finger, the pad of their finger, their fingernail, two or three fingers, and so on, until they are happy with the style and effect. For example, rubbing the screen hard with the pad of your finger creates interesting textures not achievable when drawing slender lines. Combining these different techniques allow users to create interesting shapes and letters in their unique style.

3. Tap "Ba.Net" along the top navigation to: "Clear Drawing," "Upload/Save Drawing," or return to the "Main Menu." The best way to save this image is not on this menu, but rather by taking a screenshot of the image. Press the home button and the sleep button at the same time, and a screenshot will be saved to the **Photo Roll**. Then, participants can import this image into **PS Express** or **Snapseed** for additional modification. Give them ample time to explore the image editing settings and the effects, as well as the ability to add additional text to the images.

4. After 15 minutes, ask participants to pair up and give each other feedback about their logos. Is the image clear? Are the colors effective in "selling" or promoting a product or service? Does the viewer know which product or service is being represented by this logo? Why or why not? How does it compare to the logos we explored in **LogoCheater** at the beginning of the program?

To extend this program, add a watermark option. When users have created their final logo image, give them the option to watermark it. Explain that watermarks are digital stamps that imprint over an image and are not easily cropped out or otherwise altered. A good example is what wedding photographers do when they watermark the images so wedding guests and family have to buy official prints from the photographer instead of just downloading the watermarked versions and printing them at home.

1. Open **iWaterFree**. Tap "Select Photo" to choose the desired logo image to watermark. Users can then tap "Watermarks" in the center of the bottom navigation bar to select a premade watermark, such as "Confidential" or a stamp of Picasso's signature or an image of lightening or a soccer ball.

2. Direct participants to make their own graphic watermark by tapping "Edit," and then choosing "Image." They can then pick another image, or even the logo image itself to make into a transparent watermark. Select the desired image, and a mostly-transparent version of that image will appear on the logo image in **iWaterFree**. Users can pinch/pull to resize the watermark image and move it around with their fingertip.

3. In addition to using a premade graphic watermark, direct users to try making their own text watermark (selection from the home screen) or a QR code watermark. Or they can scan a copy of their signature (black on white paper seems to work the best) using the camera. They can then add their signature as a watermark to their logo image. If using a text watermark, users can edit and define many styles, including font, size, opacity, color, and angle.

4. Give participants plenty of time to refine and perfect their watermarked logo. When they are done, tap "Save" and "Exit." They can name the file and tap save to save the image to the photo roll. From there, these images can be emailed, printed, or shared online.

NOTE

1. http://digitalyouth.ischool.berkeley.edu/report

6

Programs for Adult Audiences

LOCAL RESOURCES FOR NEW AMERICANS

Goal: To orient new members of your community—especially anyone who has recently moved from another country or region of the world—to local resources. This will give them an advantage in identifying and evaluating information and service resources in your community.

Apps: Safari, Google Maps, Yelp, Maps, Pages (optional)

Planning Note: Before you begin the program, identify some vital and practical, local resources. These should include but are not limited to:

- Libraries, especially if you are a multi-branch system.
- Hospitals, health clinics, and pharmacies; include any free places that offer blood pressure, diabetes, asthma, STD or HIV testing, cholesterol screenings, hearing or vision screenings, and free or low-cost vaccinations; include also any local organizations or service agencies who work with lesbian, gay, bisexual, or transgender adults or teens.
- Grocery stores, farmers markets, ethnic food shops, and other food resources.
- Schools, and any parent-school association from which parents can receive additional support.
- Social service referral agencies, such as children and family services, emergency help lines, domestic violence shelters, teen-centered services, etc.
- Banks, post offices, city or town hall or county office, etc.
- Emergency services; remember that not all countries have emergency 911 telephone services, and if they do, it is probably not "911."

From *iPads in the Library: Using Tablet Technology to Enhance Programs for All Ages* by Joel A. Nichols. Santa Barbara, CA: Libraries Unlimited. Copyright © 2013.

• Religious institutions, such as mosques, synagogues, churches or meetings; be sure to keep a light touch on this one, especially before you get input from participants in your program. Let users needs dictate the resources identified in this program.

Instructions:

1. Use the **Safari** app to find and bookmark some online resources in each category. Show users how to navigate various options for changing website language, if available. This is a great place to demonstrate basic iPad use tips, especially how to select text, copy and paste it into another app.

2. Identify the address to any particular agency or resource. Tell users that they will copy that text, and then paste it into the **Maps** application for directions. Press down on the text with a fingertip. A blue field with blue dots on each side will appear over a section of text or over the website.

3. Direct users to gently and precisely change the dimensions of the blue selection field to isolate just the text they want to copy and paste. Then they should select "Copy," which is a small text box hovering above the selection field.

4. Show them how to switch to **Maps**. Press the home button and then tap **Maps**. Demonstrate how to use the four-finger swipe from the bottom of the screen for fast switching, or to four/five-finger swipe to the left to change between open apps. In **Maps**, tap "Directions." In the first field, type "*current location*" or the library's address. Tell users that they can enter their own home address if they wish. In the second field, tap and press down with your fingertip in the blank area. Three options will pop up: select, select all, and paste. Direct users to tap "Paste," and the address text they copied from **Safari** will paste into the window. The screen will refresh with a new route to that address.

5. Next, demonstrate **Yelp**. Tap "OK" to allow it to use your current location. **Yelp** prefers users to have accounts, but it is not necessary for this program. Tap "No" on the first screen and then tap "Sign in later" on the second screen to get to the app features. This app collates reviews of businesses, restaurants, and other services. Users have three views to choose from—list, map, or photos. Users can search for any kind of business or service. Encourage them to use a sample, nonthreatening search such as "Restaurants" to demonstrate the service.

6. "List" shows business names, addresses, brief descriptions, and the number of stars the business has been rated. In addition, the number of reviews is listed. "Map" shows these business locations on a local map. To see the name, star rating, and number of reviews, click any of the numbered pins on the map. The photo view shows a picture of these businesses in a grid, also with the star rating and number of reviews. Tap any photo to see a photo slideshow of the business, if available.

7. Next, direct users to tap "Filter." This lets them sort results by best match, by distance, or by rating. There are preset distance radii, as well as four price levels to sort by cost. Users can also select "Open now" in this filter to see which businesses are currently listed as open. (Let them know that this information can go out of date quickly, so they should still call ahead.)

Allow plenty of time for users to search for local resources and services they need or are interested in. Be sure to include things like discussion groups, book groups, Alcoholics Anonymous, or other self-help groups as needed.

This program is most useful when users can leave with a printed handout of local resources. This could be prepared in advance, or incorporated into part of the program where users cut and paste information into a **Pages** document and then print it to make their own.

End the program by asking participants to identify any other resources they already know about but that did not come up in the program. These might be specific cultural, linguistic, or religious social service or support resources little own outside of given communities, or they might be broader word-of-mouth resources that are not easily captured in Internet searches or in **Yelp**'s search criteria. In new immigrant communities, poor communities, or unwired communities, there may be many major services and resources with little or no online presence. Do not forget to include them if you can. Consider adding these new resources to the handout so your audience can return to the library and pick it up.

ENGLISH CONVERSATION PRACTICE

Goals: To help anyone in your community interested in improving their English skills to access digital tools to help them learn and practice English conversation or grammar skills. In addition, some of these techniques can be adapted to English speakers interested in learning or practicing a foreign language.

Apps: Mango Languages, Stitcher, YouTube, iTunes U

Planning Notes: This program works best as a series of programs, which allow participants to work at their own pace over a sequence of several days or weeks. Ahead of time, make a generic **Stitcher** account for this program. Also before the program, identify appropriate material in **iTunes U**. This should be done before the program because you will need to use iTunes usernames and passwords to download even the free course content.

Books/Other Materials: English grammar or language learning materials from your collection; headphones for each participant

Instructions:
Use **Stitcher.** This app requires a user account, so ahead of time, log into with a generic **Stitcher** account created for the program. Direct users to search for "English as a Second Language" in the search bar on the upper right. This search returns relevant and useful results. The first two are "Learn English Funcast" and "English as a Second Language Podcast," both of which contain short episodes designed with ESL learners in mind. In all, these short podcast episodes add up to hours and hours of ESL content, and there is plenty for users to explore.

Tap "English as a Second Language Podcast." In the lower part of the screen, pick any episode and tap it to listen. Also of interest is the tab labeled "Listeners Also Like," which shows you what other listeners to this podcast are also listening to. This is crowd-sourced and serendipitous browsing at its best as users receive recommendations from their peers. For example, "Listeners Also Like" in this case shows a very useful podcast episode detailing the difference in use between "this morning/in the morning/on the morning," which is far too granular to appear in the broader search for English as a second language.

If you are structuring this program as a group meeting, be sure to listen to one of these podcasts all together as a group. The librarian's job is to ask clarifying and discussion questions at the end of the podcast, to define any unknown words or explain any cultural concepts missed. Allow participants to discuss as much as they want. It is great to start and end this program with this kind of group listening, and to let users explore the independent options below in between.

If your library subscribes to **Mango Languages**, a popular electronic resource, download their mobile app. You will have to make dummy accounts via the library

From *iPads in the Library: Using Tablet Technology to Enhance Programs for All Ages* by Joel A. Nichols.
Santa Barbara, CA: Libraries Unlimited. Copyright © 2013.

website first, or encourage users to use the library website (via Safari) to make their own account.

Log into **Mango Languages**. There are many English as a Second Language course modules, many of which are tasked for particular linguistic groups—English for German speakers, for Polish speakers, for Spanish speakers, for Italian speakers, etc. Show users how to pick the appropriate specific module. These can be frustrating to monolingual English librarians, because the names of these course modules are in the given language (e.g., "Inglés para hablantes de español" or "Englisch für Deutschsprachige), but users will be able to identify which they want. These are also easy to spot because the U.S. flag is the icon for all of them.

This is a great opportunity for library staff to use one of the foreign-language modules to learn a few words of some of the native languages of the participants. While they begin a Mango module, consider starting one alongside in their native language. This could help break the ice and make the program more inviting and nonthreatening, by placing yourself in the role of learner as well.

If your library does not subscribe to **Mango Languages** or another electronic language-learning service, there is still powerful, online ESL (English as a Second Language) content for you to deliver.

Open **iTunes U**. The display is an empty bookshelf. Tap "Catalog" in the upper left-hand corner to search for course content. Tap the "Categories" icon along the bottom navigation menu, and then tap "Language." Tap "See all" to display all the results in this category. So far, just Liberty University has English as a World Language and Conversation English II as options. Tap one of these course modules, and note that more information is displayed, including cost (if any—this material is largely free, but it is wise to double check), a course outline, and description of downloadable materials, or the videos and audio components available. Tap "Subscribe free" to subscribe to this course, and download any materials available.

Another useful collection is listed under "Great collections," the window under "New Courses." Find " 'You're Hired' videos" from the British Council, which contains 10 episodes with written transcripts that walk a user through the process of recruiting and hiring new staff for a company. This program is designed for ESL learners with appropriate business-level vocabulary.

This is an independent learning courseware platform, meant for self-directed learning and to support individuals. Help users download and access this content from the shelf in **iTunes U**, and then allow them to work at their own pace. Encourage them to search **iTunes U** for more relevant content. For example, users with intermediate or excellent conversational skills might want to try an introductory literature or writing class (intended for native speakers) to hone more advanced skills.

CITIZENSHIP TEST STUDY

Goals: To give participants access to information about the test for U.S. citizenship; to allow participants to take practice tests; and to determine areas of more intensive focus.

Apps: Citizenship '12, U.S. Citizenship, USCitizenship.

Books/Other Materials: Any citizenship test preparation materials from your collection; a handout highlighting http://www.uscis.gov or other resources for participants to access on their own.

Instructions:

First, have participants introduce themselves. As you go around the room, notice which participants might have more or less trouble with English-language skills. Citizenship tests include a focus on speaking, reading, and writing English. You may want to refer in this program to other resources for English conversation or writing practice.

The three apps used in this program are all free and have overlapping content. In each case, most of the content is taken directly from the 100 practice questions on the civics study materials on the website linked below.

1. Open **Citizenship '12**. Users will be asked to select their state/territory location, as well as identify the member of Congress who represents their area. This app then offers several options for test learners. From the main menu, participants can view the flash cards in order, view the flash cards in random order, view all the questions and answers, or take a practice test.
2. Tap view flashcards in order. A question will appear, "What is the supreme law of the land?" Tap the question to reveal the backside of the flashcard: "the Constitution," and swipe to the left with your fingertip to move to the next flashcard.
3. Tap "Main Menu." Select "Take a Practice Test" by tapping on it once, and then guide users through tapping the box next to the correct answer. A green checkmark will appear for the right answer, and red Xs next to the incorrect ones.
   Note—and warn participants—that in the free version of this app, it is very easy to accidentally tap one of the ads along the top or bottom banner spaces. Show users how to close the advertisement by tapping the X in the corner to return to the app.
4. Open **U.S. Citizenship**. Tap the menu icon along the bottom labeled "U.S. Citizenship HD" to advance past the welcome screen. Then chose between the three options: Practice (learning the questions), Recall (bookmarks to any questions flagged by the participants for review) or Ace it! (the practice test itself). The practice questions here are broken into several categories.
5. Tap "Practice," and then tap any of the categories. A question will appear in the top frame. Tap the bottom frame to reveal the answer. Tap the star icon in the lower right-hand corner to bookmark this question for later review. Swipe to the left to advance through the questions.

From *iPads in the Library: Using Tablet Technology to Enhance Programs for All Ages* by Joel A. Nichols.
Santa Barbara, CA: Libraries Unlimited. Copyright © 2013.

This app contains Spanish and Chinese practice modes, with the content translated. To access these language features, tap "Settings" on the bottom navigation menu. Then tap the flag of China or Spain to switch to the desired language. On this menu, participants can also enlarge the font as well as reset all questions and bookmarks.

1. Next, open **USCitizenship**. The welcome screen in this app has just three options—Start Test, Questions, and Settings—to choose the location. Tap "Settings," then tap the "State" icon on the right hand side. Choose your state, then tap anywhere outside of the Settings frame to return to the welcome screen.

2. Tap "Questions." Users can only see the first 30 questions in the free version of the app, so this app is perhaps less useful than the other two. Review whichever questions are available. They are shown in black, while the ones behind the paywall are shown grayed out.

3. Tap "Menu," and then "Home" in the upper left to return to the welcome screen. Tap "Start Test," and ask participants to take the practice test of 10 questions. A tally of right and wrong answers will be kept along the bottom of the screen.

4. Allow participants to keep studying independently with whichever app they prefer and find the most relevant. Be sure to also have available resources from your collection that might be useful, and appropriate referrals for users who wish to register for an actual test soon.

At the end of the program, be sure to steer users toward the U.S. Citizenship and Immigration Services official website at http://www.uscis.gov, for more study materials, detailed information about the tests, and information about finding help in your community. Note that this website has the Civics study materials in English as well as in Spanish and Chinese.

RESUME WORKSHOP

Goal: For participants to create updated professional-quality resumes.

Apps: ResuM8, Pages, Thesaurus

Planning Notes: Find some sample resumes online and print them out. Instruct participants to bring some information to the meeting: the dates they graduated from high school, college, or other dates; the addresses of former employers and dates employed; and phone numbers and exact titles for references.

Books/Other Materials: A sample resume; resume or cover letter books from your collection.

Instructions:
Show participants a sample resume. There are many available online or probably in your collection. Use them to create your own simple template resume for participants to practice with. These templates can be on paper or entirely digital, depending on the comfort level of your participants.

Remind everyone that the best resumes are consistent and organized. They need to come up with template structures for previous jobs or for educational attainment that stay the same. For example:

Customer Service Representative (May 2009–August 2013)
CORPORATE CALL SOLUTIONS
Gettysburg, PA

May 2009–August 2013
CUSTOMER SERVICE REPRESENTATIVE
Corporate Call Solutions, Gettysburg, PA

May, 2009–August, 2013
Customer Service Representative, Corporate Call Solutions
Gettysburg, PA

Each of these examples could work in a clear resume, and users will want to organize their information in a way that highlights or deemphasizes their information in a personal way. What is really important is maintaining the same structure throughout the resume.

Tell users about action verbs, and remind them to transform their job duties into sentences that use very active verbs. For example: instead of "responsible for answering phones, calendar and schedule, executive travel arrangements," try: "Answered phones; scheduled and maintained calendars of two senior managers; planned and purchased executive travel options."

From *iPads in the Library: Using Tablet Technology to Enhance Programs for All Ages* by Joel A. Nichols. Santa Barbara, CA: Libraries Unlimited. Copyright © 2013.

1. Open **Merriam-Webster HD Dictionary**. This dictionary doubles as a thesaurus. Demonstrate how to search by entering any action verb in the examples above into the white search bar. Point out the synonyms listed near the bottom of the entry.

2. Open **Pages**. Tap the plus sign to start a new document, and then tap "Create Document." From the next screen, chose a resume template. This document contains a "Modern Photo Letter" as well as a "Classic Resume" option. Choose the "Classic Resume" option.

3. Users can then replace the information in this template with their own. Either pair up participants to help each other proof their final products, or offer your expertise. This is also a great opportunity for a volunteer interested in helping job seekers in their community.

4. When participants have finished, they can select all the text by pressing down and selecting "Select All." Then they can change the font by tapping on the font name "Didot," in this template, and then selecting from the pop-up menu. These and other editing options—Style, List, Layout—can be accessed by tapping the paintbrush icon.

5. To check spelling, tap the wrench icon, then tap "Settings." The following menu gives users options to check spelling, word count, and other spacing guidelines.

6. Now, have users email themselves this document in three formats: Pages, PDF, and Word. They should send themselves at least the Word and PDF versions of the document. The Pages version of the file is only necessary if they have access to iPads again. To email this document, you will need to have an email account on the iPad. Consider using a generic programming email or creating one just for this kind of program.

If participants need a lot more writing help than the **Pages** template can provide, use **ResuM8**, an app that builds eye-catching, headline-based resumes. Users input their information in a form, and the tool builds a resume format. In addition, users can browse the "400 Resume Headlines" and "1000 Career Strengths" for free. More are available in the paid version.

1. Open the app.

2. Tap "Review our Proved Method" to see a sample resume written with eye-catching headlines.

3. Then users can select from the five resume content areas: contact details, career objective, major strengths, career history and education, and additional information. In each case, tap the blue bar that says "Tap to add," and a form will pop up.

4. When participants have entered all their information, they should tap "Done." At any point, you can tap "View Template" to show the resume in progress.

5. Tap the Home icon to return to the main content areas screen.

6. Tap "Share" to save and share. This app exports files via email in PDF format, as well as in RTF format (that can be easily imported to Microsoft Word), and several other cover letter options.

Offer to print resumes the participants have just created, and be sure to show users how to find the PDF or RTF versions they created and exported via email.

INTERVIEW PREP WORKSHOP

Goal: For participants to practice and record their interviewing and interpersonal skills and obtain feedback from peers.

App: Camera

Planning Note: This program works best if each participant has their own device. It can also be an effective way to involve professional volunteers seeking to help job seekers. Direct participants to bring their resume, cover letter, and a copy of the job advertisement to which they are applying. Use the sample interview questions below to model the program for participants, either at the beginning of the program or by making your own mock interview video.

Books/Other Materials: Sample resume, sample cover letter; other job hunting and interview preparation resources from your collection.

Instructions:
Start by asking the participants to introduce themselves and to say what kind of job they are applying for. Try to model a very clear introduction, and remind them to give their first and last names and to speak loudly and clearly. This will set the tone for this program and remind participants that it is to improve their interpersonal skills.

If possible, model interview answers for the crowd with a colleague. Below are some excellent sample questions to use. Adapt these or make up your own.

Before you begin, remind participants that this is just practice, and that they should focus on observing and improving their own interview style.

Sample Question:	Tell us what about your educational background or work experience makes you interested in this job?
Sample Answer:	I've always worked with cars and trucks, but decided to focus on auto body work and have been working at XYZ Motors since I graduated with an Auto Body Technician certificate in 2011. I'm interested in the position at ABC Motors because of the custom work I see coming out of this shop, and because there might eventually be room to become a supervisor.
Sample Question:	Why did you choose this field, and where do you imagine yourself in five years?
Sample Answer:	Frankly, I didn't intend on a career as an office manager. But when I started at the Walton Corporation as a receptionist, I worked with an excellent office manager who kept excellent control over a chaotic office and made my life easier. Later, when I was promoted to executive assistant and then to assistant office manager at that corporation, I realized that offering the kind of support and organization skill a good office manager does, is essential to any strong business. I found it rewarding. In five years, I hope to be managing a large office or serving as an executive assistant to a senior manager.

From *iPads in the Library: Using Tablet Technology to Enhance Programs for All Ages* by Joel A. Nichols. Santa Barbara, CA: Libraries Unlimited. Copyright © 2013.

Sample Question: Describe a particularly challenging customer service experience—internal or external customers—from your last or current job. What were the challenges and how did you overcome them?

Sample Answer: When I was teaching in an afterschool program, sometimes the parents would be very upset at their children for misbehaving in class or school, and that conflict would come into the afterschool program. In one case, Bonnie's mother was so mad that she disrupted the class and scared the other kids. I ushered her into the hall and spoke to her calmly until she calmed down. Then I helped her identify the name of Bonnie's guidance counselor from the list so she could call for more help.

There are plenty of other sample interview questions available online, and likely in your collection as well. Use them. Participants will need many examples for successful practice.

Ask participants to pair up, but note that this program works best if every participant has their own device. If someone wants to work alone, or there is an odd number, participants can ask themselves sample questions you have provided.

Participants should set up the iPad with the forward camera facing them.

1. Open **Camera**. Tap the camera icon with arrows to change which camera is in use.
2. Slide the camera mode selector from the camera icon to the video camera icon.
3. Tap the red button to begin recording, and the red light will blink. Whenever the camera is recording, a timer will also appear.
4. Ask participants to record themselves by saying hello and introducing themselves. They can watch the last video they have recorded by tapping on the small gray square in the lower left of the screen. Alternatively, show them how to access the Photo Roll to watch all the videos they have recorded.
5. After they watch their own introductions, ask them to pause for a short break. What did they already notice about themselves, if anything? Can they already start to see ways to improve their presentation?

Users who need more inspiration should review the company's website, and then record their answer to this question: What changes would you make on our company website within the first month if you were in charge of it?

Now, let the program proceed. They should take turns asking questions and recording answers, and then have plenty of time to review their videos. If you have any video content of successful interview skills in your collection, show it.

TROLLEY, TRAIN, OR TRAIL?

Figure 6.1

TransitTimes shows routes, times, and connections, such as this map of Philadelphia's Regional Rail lines. Tap any stop icon for more information.

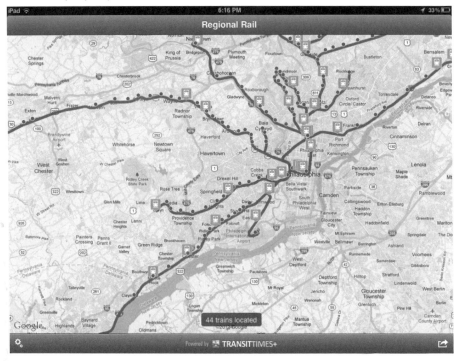

Screenshot courtesy TransitTimes

Goal: To support a successful job search or interview by helping participants plan how to get to a jobsite by mapping out a driving route, public transportation route, or ride-share options.

Apps: Maps, **Google Earth**, individual transit apps for your area if available (**New York Subway for iPad**, **Go Metro Los Angeles Version 2 or TransitTimes**, for example), **Safari**

Books/Other Materials: Local public transit timetables and maps, local maps from your collection (if available)

Instructions:
Reliable transportation is a job-hunting and job-keeping necessity, and the lack thereof usually puts low-income individuals at a disadvantage.

Make available the local maps from your collection—perhaps displaying them on a table near the group. Encourage participants to browse these as they arrive at the meeting.

From *iPads in the Library: Using Tablet Technology to Enhance Programs for All Ages* by Joel A. Nichols. Santa Barbara, CA: Libraries Unlimited. Copyright © 2013.

1. First, ask everyone to find their home address. Open **Maps** (or **Google Earth**). Direct partic-ipants to search for their home address in the app. Then use the directions function to search for the location of their interview.
2. Change the transportation mode by tapping the car icon (driving directions), the train (public transit directions), or the person (pedestrian). Google Maps gives you the option for bike directions as well, so be sure to use it if you are in a cycling community.
3. Ask participants to advance through the directions, step by step. Do they make sense? Do they already know better shortcuts to improve the route?
4. Use your city or region's public transit app, if available. This is a great example of civic lit-eracy and engagement. Be sure to also visit the websites of these transit agencies to check ticket and fare prices.

If your area has a rideshare board or online rideshare service, let participants know about it.

EFFECTIVE PRESENTATIONS

Goal: Give participants hands-on practice creating and modifying a sophisticated slide presentation and the ability to share it via email.

Apps: Keynote, Safari

Planning Notes: Although there are free slideshow viewers for the iPad, including **Prezi** and **SlideShark**, there are not comparable creation tools. To run this program using free apps only, you will have to create a presentation using Prezi or PowerPoint on a laptop or desktop computer. Then you send it to your iPad and view it using **SlideShark** or the Prezi app. **Keynote** is a powerful program developed as Apple's answer to Microsoft PowerPoint. Embed this program in an instructional setting or class visit to connect with an assignment that should be delivered via presentation. For the purposes of this program, the simple sample topic "My Favorite Restaurant" will serve as our example.

Instructions:
First, direct users to Google image search to download photos for their presentation. Remind them about copyright and include a short lesson in fair use, or search specifically for photos with Creative Commons remixing licenses. For their favorite restaurant, they might consider: images of menus, flags from the country associated with the type of food served, photographs of the kind of cuisine or other photographs that represent their restaurant. Users should save up to 10 images to use, but remind them that they may not actually be able to use them all.

1. Open **Keynote**. The app will open with one presentation already there to select, a presentation called Getting Started. This is an app tutorial—in presentation format—that users should review. It contains very specific help and a preview of **Keynote**'s most powerful features. For this sample presentation, participants will create at least one animated object and use at least one animated slide transition to demonstrate how they work. Encourage them to refer to the Getting Started guide to see other available effects and functions.
2. Tap the plus sign in the upper left corner of the screen, and then tap "Create Presentation." Pick from 1 of 12 templates with various colors and styles. A new presentation will load.
3. On the first slide, there is one photo and two text boxes that are helpfully labeled "Double-tap to edit." Tap the photo and then tap "Replace" to choose a new photo from the Photo Roll. The image on this first slide should be the best overall image that represents the theme of the presentation, the ideal vacation.
4. Direct participants to double-tap the text boxes to edit the text. When they are finished, they can tap the key in the lower right-hand corner to put away the Keyboard, or tap anywhere outside of the text box.
5. Users should also add an animation to this first picture. Tap it and then tap "Animate." Choose build-in, so the animation will happen at the beginning of the side. Build-out animates it at the end of the slide, if desired. Select a kind of animation from the list. There are several movements, as well as Flames, Sparkles, Lens Flares, and Fades, to choose from.

From *iPads in the Library: Using Tablet Technology to Enhance Programs for All Ages* by Joel A. Nichols. Santa Barbara, CA: Libraries Unlimited. Copyright © 2013.

Select one and an automatic preview will show the effect in action. To select it, tap anywhere outside the animations menu.

6. To add a new slide, tap the plus sign on the bottom of the slide viewer in the left-hand column. Participants can then choose from a variety of text and photo layouts; and they can also move around and resize any text or image by selecting it and pulling the corners. In addition, tap the plus sign in the upper right corner navigation to add other images, text boxes, other media, charts, or shapes. Scroll to the left to reveal additional shapes and colors.

7. Add an animation between slide 1 and slide 2. Tap slide 1 to select it and then tap the wrench icon in the upper right-hand navigation and then select Transitions and Builds. A small black box with an arrow pointing to slide 1 will pop up; tap the plus sign on that box to add a transition. Select the desired transition. Wait and watch the sample of that transition. Then, tap anywhere outside the box the transition menu to choose it, or select another.

8. Encourage users to make up to five slides showing their dream vacation. Remind them that the most effective presentations make use of white space and balance the amount of text and images with each other, and also with the white space. Point out slides in the "Getting Started" tutorial presentation that achieve this effectively. Also point out that while animations and transitions are fun and snazzy, they can look childish or unpolished if there are too many of them.

At the end, ask users to present their Dream Vacations to the whole group by playing through their presentation. They can them email it to themselves in one of three formats: Keynote, PowerPoint, or as a PDF file.

CRAFTERS' DIGITAL PORTFOLIO

Goals: For participants to create a picture catalog of their crafts, as a first step in starting an online store and to learn how to share pictures with friends and family.

Apps: Camera, PicStitch, Dropbox, Safari

Planning Notes: Instruct participants to bring in examples of their crafts, or to bring in JPEG photographs of their craft on a flash drive. Use a desktop computer to put these in a **Dropbox** folder, and then retrieve them from the **Dropbox** folder.

Books/Other Materials: Up to five samples of any craft work, such as knitting, crochet, sewing, felting, or cross stitch.

Instructions:
PicStitch is an app that uses preset layout templates and photo editing options to make photo collages. The app has 32 different layout grids. Each square in the layouts will have its own picture, and most of these layouts have only three, four, or five rectangles available.
    Swipe to the left to page through the template grids. Select a grid by tapping it.
    There is no in-app camera in PicStitch. Instead, instruct participants to switch to the camera apps to take pictures for their illustration.

1. Tap the "edit" icon to rotate and crop images, as well as to add text. Select the "text" icon and a transparent text box will appear over the image.
2. Import photos into all the layout grids. Return to each photo individually, and add text boxes. Label the craft with information about the object, what it is made out of and how you made it.

These collage portfolios can be exported or saved for printing and emailing, or uploading to a website or ecommerce store.

Figure 6.2
Make a collage like this one in minutes using your own photographs and **PicStitch**'s layout options.

Photos and collage by Joel A. Nichols

From *iPads in the Library: Using Tablet Technology to Enhance Programs for All Ages* by Joel A. Nichols. Santa Barbara, CA: Libraries Unlimited. Copyright © 2013.

Figure 6.3

Heredis keeps track of ancestors and organizes their important life dates into printable family tree charts.

Screenshot courtesy b.s.d. concept

Goals: To create a graphical family tree in GEDCOM file format (a standard family tree file format readable across many software applications, desktop and tablet, that can be exported for later use) and to practice searching library genealogical resources.

Apps: Heredis, Ancestry, Safari

Planning Note: Participants who already have some information about their own family tree will get more out of this program. The more information (ancestor names, birth dates, and birthplaces) they bring into the program, the more elaborate a family tree they can make. Otherwise, participants should use library resources to search for birth and death notices to start filling in theirs. Ahead of time, instruct participants to bring in any information they have about their ancestors to the session. If there are staff members at your library who already regularly provide genealogical research services or reference, ask them to help by preparing a short presentation or pathfinder.

Books/Other Materials: Sample family tree; any genealogy reference materials from your collection.

From *iPads in the Library: Using Tablet Technology to Enhance Programs for All Ages* by Joel A. Nichols. Santa Barbara, CA: Libraries Unlimited. Copyright © 2013.

Instructions:

Start this program with paper samples of a family tree. Print out a sample one by taking a screenshot from **Heredis**'s sample file, or find any family tree online or in a book to show. Then briefly introduce participants to any databases or electronic resources accessible. Many libraries and consortia subscribe to resources such as *America's Obituaries and Death Notices* or *Biography and Genealogy Master Index*.

If your library does not subscribe to any of these services, consider searching local newspapers in whatever format you can: microfilm, print, or online.

Spend several minutes showing participants how to access and search these resources using the **Safari** app. One excellent place to start is for people to search for parents or grandparents, even if they already know the information. When they see that their search strategies retrieve information they already know and trust, they can scaffold those searches better to look for ancestors they know less about.

When everyone has some number of ancestor data sets (that is, names, birth dates, and locations), direct them to open **Heredis**. Tap the long blue button labeled "New Family File," name the file, and tap "Done."

1. The following screen will be a blank family file. Notice the navigation bar at the bottom of the screen. The "Persons" icon should be highlighted. Return to the home screen by tapping "Home." The left-hand column lists each person added to the family file. Click the white plus sign in the lower right of the column to add people.

2. Direct participants to add themselves. Now, in the right-hand column, the Data window for this individual will appear. They can add photos or videos of this person by selecting "Add Media," and then should fill in the other details as they wish. There are also links to add an event, such as a birth, christening, death, or burial, as well as extended options such as adoption, mitzvah celebrations, immigration, retirements, or travel. Encourage users to add any events appropriate for their family.

3. Tap the Info- or Info+ buttons to switch between views with more or less of this kind of detail available. Direct participants to add their own siblings, partners or spouses, children, and parents. This will take several minutes. Circulate through the group and offer hands-on navigation help. They should do this by first tapping on themselves, and then tapping the "Add father" or "Add mother" buttons above their name. They can add partners and children by tapping the blue buttons underneath the box with their name.

4. When they have added at least three individuals, show participants how to change from individual record view to tree view by tapping the flow-chart icon at the top of the right-hand side. They can advance through different branches or charts by navigating with the left and right buttons at the upper right of the screen.

5. Along the bottom navigation, tap "Charts," which presents the family tree in progress graphically, superimposed on an illustration of a tree. The indexes tab allows users to input places and sources just once to use on any record they like. Fill in as much of the family tree as possible.

For serious amateur genealogists, explain that they can export this file as a GEDCOM file to use later with any number of programs. Tap tools, then "Exporting GEDCOM file," and choose email. For people interested in just a quick family tree takeaway from this program, make screenshots of their graphical charts (either the one superimposed on a tree or the traditional chart view) to print or email.

Ancestry is another app with similar functionality, and offers the ability to search LDS (Church of Jesus Christ of Latter-day Saints) historical records automatically to help user fill out their searches. This app is somewhat more visual and graphically user-friendly, and enables full family tree views as well as views that only show direct ancestors. Encourage participants who are already registered on Ancestry.com to use this app instead of Heredis. This app allows users to publish their family trees (by making them public online), but does not export a GEDCOM file.

EREADER PROGRAM

Goal: To introduce an adult audience to downloading and reading eBooks. This program is meant to demonstrate how users can download eBooks, and is structured around accessing free eBooks in the public domain. Depending on what vendors supply your library and what formats are available to download, adapt this program accordingly to include showing users to how download eBooks.

Apps: iBooks, Kobo, Kindle (optional), **OverDrive Media Console** (optional), **Nook** (optional), **Google Books** (optional).

Planning Notes: To use **iBooks**, you may have to authenticate the iTunes account with the password, so change the password to something easy to input or be ready to enter it for participants.

Instructions:

Start this program by explaining that there are many books available for free, many of which come without the Digital Rights Management (DRM) restrictions of online stores like Amazon's Kindle store or Barnes & Noble's Nook, which encodes the file so it cannot be copied or shared. While these free books include many older classics, it also includes the works of contemporary authors who have licensed their work under Creative Commons licenses, such as Cory Doctorow, Charles Stross, and Lawrence Lessig.

1. First, demonstrate **Kobo**. This free reader offers instant download to free popular books and novellas as well as a variety of classics via Project Gutenberg. **Kobo** can also support any e-pub format eBook from a library catalog. Tap any book cover to download the content. Tap "Library" or "recent" to see recent downloads, and then swipe to turn the pages. There are options along the lower right hand side to change text size and style, screen brightness and white on black vs. black on white contrast.

2. Next, open **iBooks**. Its interface looks like an empty bookshelf. To find books to add to your shelf, tap "Library" in the upper left-hand corner. Then tap the browse icon along the bottom navigation menu. This loads a browsable menu on the left-hand column and the option to sort paid and free books by author last name. Tap "Free." Have users select an author from the list. There are many literary classics and popular genre classics, such as Zane Grey, as well as more contemporary works by Kurt Vonnegut, Philip K. Dick, and Ted Dekker. Tap the "Free" button next to the book, which will then turn into a green "Get book" button. Note here that you will need to authorize with an iTunes password associated with the iPad, so be ready to do that for users, or temporarily change the password to something easy to input.

3. Enter the password and click "OK." The screen will then automatically resolve back to the bookshelf, and you will see the eBook you just downloaded. Explore the reading and display options with users by tapping the controls in the upper right hand of the screen: an icon to resize the text, change the brightness, font, and style; a magnifying glass icon that accesses a search function to look for a specific phrase or page number; and a bookmark icon. Tap it to mark your spot.

From *iPads in the Library: Using Tablet Technology to Enhance Programs for All Ages* by Joel A. Nichols. Santa Barbara, CA: Libraries Unlimited. Copyright © 2013.

4. Now, demonstrate how to check out and download a library eBook. If patrons are interested, you could also give them pointers about shopping and paying for books on a various commercial website or via a one of the commercial apps.

ADAPTIVE TOOLS

Goals: To show seniors or other beginning users how to adjust the iPad's accessibility settings, and to show them the ways people with visual or hearing impairments can use the device.

Apps: Settings, **eReader app** or **Safari** (if desired)

Books/Other Materials: This program is a perfect time to feature items from your large print and audiobook collections.

Instructions:
Open **Settings**. Tap "General." Scroll down with a fingertip to Accessibility, and tap on it. Adaptations for people with visual impairments are all located in this menu with on/off toggle switches. Toggle VoiceOver on. This speaks the name of whatever a fingertip touches.

Note that this option turns two-finger down/up scroll into three fingers for that scroll. Be sure to use three fingers, or you will find navigation in VoiceOver mode sluggish and unresponsive. Use a flick gesture instead of a single tap, as well.

Tap **VoiceOver**. This menu shows the various options for this tool, including whether to give feedback typing out loud, to speak hints, or to change the speaking rate. There are 37 language options for this VoiceOver, too. In addition, a more sophisticated control gesture called the Rotor can be enabled. Enable the rotor by twisting the fingers against the screen as though you were twisting a dial. This control allows users to move through web or document content in very granular ways, including going character by character, word by word, line by line, or even link by link.

Users can also choose Zoom, Large Text, and White on Black to enhance visibility, or Speak Selection and Speak Auto-text to replace the visual with audio output.

There are less developed options for Hearing (just changing the audio from one ear to the other) and for Physical and Motor impairments. Tap Adaptive touch if users have difficulty touching the screen.

The final option, Triple-click Home, lets users switch automatically to: VoiceOver, White on Black, Zoom, or AssistiveTouch by pressing the home button three times. Enable this option if you have regular users who prefer using the device with these adaptations.

1. For this program, select "Toggle Zoom." If desired, direct users to open **Safari** or an **eReader app**, and have them turn on Zoom inside the app by triple-clicking the home button. Does it work? Do the apps you are using have the ability to enlarge text?
2. Switch back to Settings.
3. Toggle VoiceOver on.
4. Switch back to the Safari page or to the eReader: how does it perform? Does it read the screen aloud?

Let participants come together at the end of the program to discuss their experiences and to share tips with each other. What made the devices more or less usable? What other features do they need to use the tablet effectively?

From *iPads in the Library: Using Tablet Technology to Enhance Programs for All Ages* by Joel A. Nichols.
Santa Barbara, CA: Libraries Unlimited. Copyright © 2013.

BRAIN GAMES

Goal: To show seniors several games on the iPad that are easy and fun to play and intended for users to improve their swiping dexterity and memory.

Apps: Brainquest, Watch That!, BalloonPopper, Sporcle

Planning Notes: This program works best in an open access style, where a librarian demonstrates several apps and then lets users continue along with minimal supervision or help (although the librarian should float among the participants, offering help and encouragement).

Instructions:

1. Demonstrate **Brainquest**. This trivia game contains questions at different levels for grades one through five. Even with older users though, start using the questions intended for young audiences. Let participants know that the questions will be goofy, but that they are the best way to practice using the device.
2. Next, Demonstrate **Watch That!** Tap "New game." A series of numbers inside circles appear. Memorize their locations and then tap any circle. The numbers disappear and the user must tap them in ascending order. As users progress, the number of circles increases, becoming more challenging.
3. **BalloonPopper** is an app that helps users to exercise their tapping fingers. Tap "Kids," especially if your users are slower, have dexterity problems, or are quick to be frustrated. Balloons begin rising in the play space, and users must tap them to pop them. When users pop any color balloon except black, they earn a point.

The balloons come quickly, and it is not possible to pop them all. Encourage participants to use all of their fingers!

Sporcle has a series of trivia games on different topics. They are created by many different users, so be sure to preview which games you will offer to the public. Direct users to select a **Sporcle** trivia quiz of their choice and to complete it. Simply type the answers. Any right answer is automatically accepted by the app and the user will see it appear on the Sporcle game interface.

VIRTUAL MUSEUM VISITS

Figure 6.4
Design Museum's liquid grid slides over itself to reveal more objects from its collection and gives participants control over how the app appears to them. This control makes for a more pleasurable and engaged user experience.

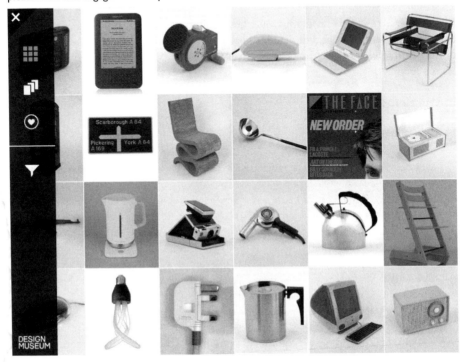

Screenshot courtesy Design Museum

Goal: To offer seniors a social/cultural experience together in pairs or small groups by accessing great collections of art. In the process, they will gain valuable iPad skills such as monitoring volume, brightness, and switching between apps.

Apps: MoMa AB EX NY (MoMA Abstract Expressionism New York), **The Getty Art in L.A. HD**, **The Louvre HD**, **The National Gallery HD**, **Design Museum Collection**, **Safari**

Planning Notes: This program takes participants through four museums via their mobile apps, and then offers them time to explore on their own. Two of these apps have substantial audio content, so headphones could come in handy if anyone is participating by themselves and/or has difficulty hearing.

Books/Other Materials: Travel books about museums; art books featuring specific museum collections; headphones (optional).

From *iPads in the Library: Using Tablet Technology to Enhance Programs for All Ages* by Joel A. Nichols. Santa Barbara, CA: Libraries Unlimited. Copyright © 2013.

Instructions:

1. Start with the **Design Museum** collection. Not only is it an excellent collection of objects, but it also features a sophisticated app interface that in and of itself is an example of excellent design.

2. Demonstrate how the grid of objects scrolls up and down and left and right. Then ask users to pick something that catches their eye. From bicycles to computer mice, teapots to the Kindle, these objects all tell an interesting story about consumer culture and design.

3. Pick an object. It will expand to fill the screen. Tap on the picture, and a series of pictures of the object from different angles will pop up. To return to the object page, tap the orange X in the upper left.

4. Each object is described in a short article, and there is also an accompanying video from museum staff for each object. Return to the main grid of exhibited objects by clicking on the plus sign in the upper left, and then the grid icon. Users can use the heart icon to mark certain objects as favorites.

5. Ask participants which of the filter categories (Architecture, Furniture, Graphics, Products, and Transportation) they are most interested in and narrow the exhibition. Do this by tapping the filter icon. The last set of icons in the left-hand navigation ribbon is a link to every object in the exhibition. This is another access point, which lists all 60 objects in a row and has a small, thumbnail picture of each.

6. Open **The Louvre HD**. Paintings are organized by century (somewhat inconveniently labeled with Roman numerals) or by name of the painter. Change this filter by tapping on the buttons on the lower left. Paintings can be displayed in thumbnail form or in a list that also displays the title. When a user wants a closer look at a painting, they just tap to select and the larger size is visible. Users can tap the "I" icon to see basic information about the painting, including the year it was painted. This text enlarges when users tap on the A+ icon on the bottom right.

    The app also includes a slideshow, and it comes with three classical music tracks that will play while the user browses the art collection. Inside the menu on the left-hand side, tap music. A music player window will pop up with three selections. Press "Play" and show the participants to use the paddle buttons on the side of the iPad to adjust the volume. Prompt users to look around, and to use the star icon to mark their favorite paintings for later.

7. Then, open **The National Gallery HD**. It is the same app design as the Louvre app, and it is hard to tell them apart. There is a key filter difference: this collection is also sortable by genre and can be further refined by name of the artist within the genre.

8. Next, this program turns to modern art, and to museums in the United States. **The Getty Exhibition** provides a long glimpse into Los Angeles art. There are four parts of the exhibition, and the works of art are sortable by work name and artist, and additionally by style and material. Prompt users to search for a genre, such as pop art or political art, or a medium such as photography or sculpture/ceramics. There are also several audio features. Try Diane Arbus's "A Castle in Disneyland," which will be most recognizable to your audience in terms of artist and subject.

9. Next, demonstrate the **Museum of Modern Art's Abstract Expressionism in New York** exhibition app. Browse by artist or by year, which makes it easy to see how styles have changed over time. Searching by year also allows participants to find a way to connect their own lives to these works of art. Prompt them to talk about what they were doing during these years.

10. Demonstrate the five-fingered bottom-up swipe to move between apps, so they can jump from museum to museum as they like. Conclude this program by giving participants as much time as they like to explore these various collections. Encourage them to write a postcard about their favorite painting or object, or to check out a book related to an artist or art that interests them. Use the screenshot feature to print or email users' favorite images, or use these printouts to make the postcard suggested above.

With more advanced users, consider using the **Kayak** app to price hypothetical trips to one of these museums. Tap "Flights," and then enter a departure and destination. Be sure to pick dates in the future.

Be sure to include any local online exhibitions, inside or outside your library, that participants can access via **Safari**. Be sure to test them before the program to make sure the given digital exhibition displays and loads correctly on the iPad. (Remember, websites that use Flash will not display; some online exhibitions are coded with Flash.)

VISUAL RECIPE POT LUCK

Goal: To turn a regular recipe into an audiovisual recipe to share. If desired and appropriate for your community, turn this into a family potluck!

Apps: Camera, Epicurious, VoiceThread

Planning Notes: Ask participants to make their favorite dish before the program and take several pictures of the food in preparation. They can bring these pictures to the program in electronic format or email them in. If they bring them in on USB sticks, have a desktop or laptop computer available for physical transfer. If there is an iPad camera connector available, users could bring in their digital cameras to transfer the photos. If desired, make this into an actual potluck dinner and instruct participants ahead of time to bring their finished dish to share.

Books/Other Materials: Cookbooks to feature from your collection; iPad camera connector (optional).

Instructions:

This program is easily adapted in a classroom situation, or where a library has a kitchen that is open for public use or cooking instruction. Split the group in two, one to cook the recipe, and one to document it via these methods. Switch roles for a second recipe.

Open **VoiceThread**. Tap the plus sign to start a new project. Import the photos by tapping the Library or take them with the **Camera**.

1. Tap "New comment" on the bottom navigation menu and then the first slide image.
2. Tap the "ABC" to add the list of ingredients.
3. Then tap the Microphone icon. Now the user should narrate making the entire recipe. They should describe each image and can advance to the next by tapping the white arrow in the lower right.
4. After users are happy with the voice-over, they can return to any individual image in their slideshow to add a text caption.
5. Tap the blue Save button.
6. To share, tap the mail icon on the upper right. Be sure to ask participants permission before sharing their recipes or their email address.

Consider setting up a generic library email address and then sharing the links to the new voice thread to participants later via blind carbon copy.

If desired, direct your audience to bring in a finished dish, as well as the pictures, for a potluck dinner.

From *iPads in the Library: Using Tablet Technology to Enhance Programs for All Ages* by Joel A. Nichols. Santa Barbara, CA: Libraries Unlimited. Copyright © 2013.

HEADLINE DISCUSSION

Goal: To read, listen, or watch news and then discuss current events in a group setting. This program is great for seniors or others who are in the library every morning.

Apps: AP Mobile, BBC News, Stitcher, Qwiki, Noticias, Telemundo

Planning Notes: This program is easily adapted to a classroom setting. Ask students to read articles on the same topics from different sources for a quick, hands-on exercise about journalistic bias and point of view. Or, use the social media sharing options inside these apps to help the class curate a social media presence about current events. Consider finding resources in other languages, even if you do not speak the language. There are several listed above for Spanish-speaking users. Put all of these apps inside a News folder. Press on one of them until they are all blinking. Drag it atop another news app, which will create a folder you can rename to "News." Drag the rest of the apps in. This will make it easier for participants to find and switch between these apps.

Instructions:

1. Open **AP Mobile**. The home screen will display a top article, and then a horizontal bar of pictures of other top news. Select the top article, scroll horizontally to see photos of others, or scroll down to see the photo and first paragraph of the article.
2. Tap the settings (gear) icon in the upper right and then tap "Font size" to make the type bigger and more readable.
3. Tap the menu button. in the upper left to display categories, including Big Stories, Local News, and Photos and Videos, as well as Showbiz, World, Oddities, Technology, etc.
4. Ask everyone to pick an article and read it. In about five minutes, ask them to report on the article. Moderate a discussion, and encourage participants to pass around their iPad to share the stories.
5. Open **BBC News**. There is an easy to navigate grid of 16 top stories in four categories. Users can scroll each row to the left to display more stories. Many stories have video content. This app also has a live radio option, located in the upper right, for any users having trouble participating because of the reading involved. There are also options (-A and A+) to decrease and increase the font size located in the upper right of the app.
6. After 10 minutes of reading and exploring, bring everyone back to discussion. What did they learn? Did they find an article about the same topic on the **BBC News** app? If not, what else caught their interest?
7. Identify any issue around which the group's interest coalesces. Discuss it, and use it as a search term to find additional content.
8. Open **Stitcher**. This app provides radio content. Ahead of time, you should log into each app with a generic **Stitcher** account created for the program. This app contains thousands of hours of audio content, so you will have to guide users to specific results they can consume within the program time frame, say 20 or 30 minutes. One surefire way is to search news in the search box in the upper right. The top results are mainstream news outlets such as Fox and ABC, as well as world, international, technology and other news.

From *iPads in the Library: Using Tablet Technology to Enhance Programs for All Ages* by Joel A. Nichols. Santa Barbara, CA: Libraries Unlimited. Copyright © 2013.

9. Allow users to explore some of this content, and then report back. If there is a specific issue identified above, search for it and play the content aloud. If not, allow users to choose. Provide headphones for anyone who needs them, but this program works best if, by this point, everyone wants to listen to the same news to discuss.

10. **Qwiki** is a reference app with limited scope but very engaging, photo-heavy interface for ready reference and news. Tap "News." Swipe to the left to see all the media, or advance with the slide ribbon along the bottom of the screen. Tap the +Q icon on the bottom menu to see related topics, with maps, images, and audio clips. Tap the back icon to return to the previous topic, or search the database via the search bar in the upper right. It is a versatile app that can help adapt this program to many ages.

11. The interfaces of **Noticias Univision** and **Telemundo 47** (Spanish-language news sources) are similarly structured. In Noticias Univision, select a category such as "Lo Ultimo" (latest news) or other. **Telemundo 47** also has a left-hand navigation and is more popular in entertainment and New York local news. Pair it with the information in Qwiki for a bilingual audience. El País, a world newspaper in Spanish, is designed much more like a traditional newspaper, with three columns and no audio or video content.

7

Program Evaluation Tips

If your use of iPads is new or part of a pilot program, you will definitely need program evaluation tools to show the impact of these programs on audiences. Even if you are not piloting a program, use the options below to evaluate and document your programs, and to improve them via participant feedback.

MEDIA CREATED

One evaluation measure is the media created. Whenever possible, follow the advice in the program plans to save and export any media or projects created by program participants to feature on your library's website or social media pages, or in grant reports or applications. These products will dramatically demonstrate the value of these programs in teaching users new skills as well as in creating web content for the library.

If you have patrons unwilling to sign releases that allow you to publish these projects, export and save the files as internal examples, or modify them and make them anonymous and unidentifiable to the creators. This will enable you to have internal examples to show supervisors, directors, funders, or board members.

ATTENDANCE AND CIRCULATION

Be sure to keep track of program attendance as well as program length. It is easy to keep track of these statistics during the program if you are using an instructor iPad, and to document the program with photographs of the program in action for reports. Always have a collection of traditional media, like books and DVDs related to the materials covered in your iPad program. Encourage participants to checkout these materials out to home the skills offered in the training. Then track your circulation at the times you are offering programs to be able to record any increases. One other way to create concrete deliverables from iPad programs that you can use for both internal and external audiences is to video record enthusiastic participants doing public service announcement-style testimonials about the program.

SURVEYS

Consider using a survey delivered on the iPad. The simplest and cheapest ways are to use web tools and apps that allow you to create a survey on your laptop or desktop, which can then be delivered via iPad.

If you have Wi-Fi access in your program, use Google forms to create a survey, and then access that survey in Safari via link. Bookmark that page by tapping the arrow coming out of a box icon, and then tap "Add to Home Screen." This sends the Safari bookmark to your iPad home screen, and makes it easy for users to access the survey the same way they would open an app, by tapping it.

Another web tool to try is **QuickTapSurvey**. Download the app, and then follow the link to http://www.quicktapsurvey.com to register a free account. This account must be activated via email verification. Once you are registered, you can create surveys using the web tool via any common browser. When you have finished writing the survey, open the app again and click surveys to find the one you authored on your computer. This survey app is more dynamic and easier for users to use than Google forms.

Consider asking questions about previous iPad or tablet use or ownership to gauge the extent to which users have access to these devices at home or at school. For each program, ask questions about the literacy goals identified in the program plan. For example, are users more comfortable making graphs? Did they learn more about the solar system? Can they article properties of effective logo designs, app interface designs, or effective presentations? Are they more comfortable and feel more prepared for their job interview? Would they recommend this program to a friend, why or why not?

In addition, use these surveys with open-ended questions. Ask what the best part of the program was and what the worst was. Ask what users would most like to change or add to the program. The mixture of qualitative and quantitative responses will help you refine and improve the program delivery for next time.

In both cases, the web interfaces of these two tools have analytical capabilities to collect and tabulate responses, as well as display the information graphically in charts or graphs. If it is not feasible to deliver the surveys on the iPad, use paper. Use the graphing capabilities in **Keynote** or **Pages** to make effective presentations of your programming data.

Appendix A

85 Essential Apps for Library Programming

Note: This list contains the apps described in the preceding pages, as well as others useful in a library setting.

123DSCULPT (free): A 3D sculpture and design app that gives users a lump of virtual clay or several premade shapes to alter. Users can rotate the view in all directions and can interact with the virtual clay much as they would with actual modeling clay.

3D CellStain (free): A set of interactive graphics and microscope photography that display and show the structure and parts of a cell.

7 Billion ($4.99): Published by the National Geographic Society, this app features photography, informational text, interactive maps, videos, and more all about the impact of a rising human population on Earth. Use these high-quality images to illustrate or inspire research projects and for sparking group discussions.

AP Mobile (free): This app delivers breaking news content from the Associated Press. Users can search for particular stories or themes, or see headline news in several categories. Contains text and photo content.

Arctic Watch (free): This app is powered by NASA satellite data that shows the yearly seasonal ice melt at the Arctic and Antarctic; historical data shows up to 30 years of ice data for comparison.

BBC News (free): Delivering international news from the British Broadcasting Company (BBC) in text, audio, and video formats, this app connects users to many kinds of world news.

BoboExploresLight ($4.99): An interactive science textbook with stunning illustrations that follow a little creature, Bobo, through experiences about the science of light, such as photosynthesis, color, and so on.

Crayola LCC (Lights, Camera, Color!) ($1.99): This app creates a digital coloring page by draining any photograph of color but maintaining the lines. It has an in-app camera, or users can upload from the photo roll to quickly remove the color from any image, and then color it on the screen with virtual crayons, markers, or pencils.

Creatures of Light (free): Reference app from the American Museum of Natural History about kinds of bioluminescence, how it works, and how bioluminescent organisms are studied. The text is fairly dense, explaining scientific concepts at levels appropriate for middle schoolers and above, but also has lots of engaging and vivid photographs.

CutTheRope ($0.99): This app is an educational game incorporating principles of physics in a dynamic and interactive play space. Users move through a series of challenges in which the goal is getting a cookie in a frog's mouth, and they must conceptualize and experiment with force, velocity, direction, gravity, etc. It takes a very long time for children and young teens to tire of this game!

Design Museum (free): Digital museum of objects from the collections of the Design Museum of London, presented in a slick and liquid interface that is, itself, as innovative as some of the art on display. Each object in this digital collection has a complete catalog record with detailed information.

DoodleBuddy (free): Simple paint app with preset backgrounds, stamps, and stencils to make more powerful images; contains tools to draw circles and squares.

Dropbox (free): Seamlessly share photos, documents, and other files between the iPad and any other computer or device; set up public folders to share large files too big to email.

EarthObserver ($0.99): This app, developed at Columbia University, feeds many kinds of earth science and climate data onto interactive maps of Earth from a variety of governmental and scientific sources, including NASA, USGS, and others. Practice geolocation of data, compare climate data in different parts of the world, and use this app for excellent examples of enhanced maps.

Educreations Interactive Whiteboard (free): A digital whiteboard for working out problems that includes a text tool and 10 different colored markers to choose from.

Epicurious (free): This app is compendium of easy-to-follow recipes with rich photographs and options to search by cuisine or ingredient.

Exploriments: Electrostatics–Coulomb's Law ($2.99): Interactive electricity experiments with clear illustrations.

Exploriments: Fluids–Archimedes Principle, Buoyancy and Flotation ($3.99): Interactive science experiments about fluid science.

Exploriments: Weight, Mass and Force of Gravity–Effect of Altitude and Comparison across Multiple Planets (free): Six interactive science experiments about weight, mass, and gravity.

Felt Board ($2.99): Create compelling felt scenes with predesigned characters and shapes. Keep interactive for one-on-one play or use it to create visuals for a digital storytime, which can be shared via the in-app screenshot tool. Colors are bright and attractive, and the art emulates the texture of real felt.

Flipboard (free): Curate your own iPad magazine with this app; pull in content from your social media feeds or from other blogs and magazines to create a digital magazine with custom content.

Fotobabble (free): This app allows users to add voice-over content or text content to one image or a series of images. Use it to create a narrated slideshow or a talking postcard that you can email.

GarageBand ($4.99): Apple's proprietary music creation app; powerful virtual instrument emulators and mixing capabilities.

The Getty Art in L.A. HD (free): This app tells the story of the history of art in Los Angeles from 1945 to 1980 and is made up of four different digital exhibitions. Users can listen to audio content and see painting, photographs, sculpture, and other art presented in an information-rich environment.

Getty Images (free): A catalog of stock photos that make excellent writing prompts and illustrations; users can search, browse, save, and share some 24 million photos, as claimed by the app. Shake the iPad for a random picture.

Google Earth (free): Google's powerful mapping and satellite imaging data are at your fingertips in this app; includes 3D recreations of some cities as well as views inside famous buildings and landmarks. This is a must-have reference app.

Greenpeace Images (free): Beautiful and high-interest photography of nature from an environmentalist organization; often updated content brings world from the rainforest to the Antarctic, as they advertise, to the iPad.

iBloom (free): Users grow a virtual flower or virtual vegetable plant in this app, which includes interactive motions to supply the plants with their basic needs: food, water, and air. For example, users blow into the microphone to give their plant air.

iMotion HD (free): Make stop-motion animated films with just a few taps. The in-app settings allow users to control the frame capture speed as well as the playback speed to achieve desired stop motion effects, and the app uses an onlon-skin translucent image option to keep your objects exactly where you mean them to be.

iMovie ($4.99): Apple's proprietary video editing application that brings nearly professional-grade editing functionality to home and educational users. Users can create, edit, and share HD movies.

i Tell a Story ($0.99): An easy-to-use podcasting tool that allows users to record audio of any kind and enhance it with sound effects on a simple three-track mixing deck.

iTranslate Voice ($0.99): This app is a translation machine to and from 24 major world languages and their dialects; speak into the microphone and the software translates, and it speaks back a reply. Users can also correct the input by using the in-app keyboard.

Job Aware (free): Although this app is primarily a tool to search for job ads, it also comes with helpful content about writing resumes, researching companies, and effective interviewing, as well as offering a salary comparison tool across 50 U.S. cities.

Jurassic Park (free): This dinosaur-keeping game features simple graphics; users feed, water, and build enclosures as they manage a dinosaur zoo. Similar to iBloom in concept.

Keynote ($9.99): iOS's answer to Microsoft PowerPoint is easy to use and comes with built-in animations and transitions that spice up presentations. Keynote can open and export Power-Point (.ppt) format files as well. The multitouch interface is well suited for presentation making, and this app can be easier to use than a mouse-and-keyboard desktop version.

Kindle (free): Amazon's proprietary ereading app, which allows users to download and read Kindle format books (.azw and .KF8). While most of the content is paid, the app is free, and any libraries using OverDrive's eBook service will have access to Kindle format books. In addition, Amazon does offer some free content, especially preview chapters.

LeafSnap HD (free): This ultimate electronic field guide is used to identify trees by photographing their leaves; users take a photograph and then work through the database to match it to a species.

Lego 4+ (free): This app is a simple driving game constructed in the style of a classic progressive landscape video game like the original Mario Brothers. Users must first tap together different Lego parts to create more complicated Lego vehicles, which they can then use in the game to collect coins as they drive along the landscape. There are also puzzle levels with more complicated Lego objects and scenes to construct.

LEGO Photo (free): An easy-to-use photo app that turns any image into a photo mosaic that looks like it is made of Legos. Users can tap their mosaic to change to different color schemes.

Letters A to Z ($0.99): An app designed for very young children to practice their letter knowledge and phonological awareness skills; users tap a letter to hear its name and tap pictures of objects that animate and play the sound of the letter.

Letter Tracer ($0.99): This simple app is based on a Montessori technique for children to practice writing letters. There are options that allow children to trace an outlined letter and also copy the letter without the tracing guide.

Literacy Skills Sampler HD (free): This app is designed for adults who wish to improve their functional literacy skills. Short videos isolate and highlight basic words, using lots of visuals. Design is bright and clear without being childish or simplistic.

Loopcam (free): This app is a photo and camera tool that allows users to take up to 50 still photos, which the app then animates into a loop. Great for making popular animated GIFs for Tumblr or sharing on other social network services.

The Louvre HD (free): A digital subset of the Louvre's iconic collections, accompanied by short informational articles about the painting.

MapBox (free): A powerful mapping tool that draws on many open-source products to provide sophisticated map making, viewing, and sharing capabilities.

Mars Globe (free): An interactive globe that rotates, spins, and zooms to and from the surface of Mars seamlessly; follow a guided tour or visit over 1,500 geographical features on your own with links to more information.

Merriam Webster Dictionary (free): This is an easy-to-use and authoritative dictionary that offers pronunciation help and synonyms and antonyms in addition to definitions.

Miniatures (free): This video tool creates tilt-shift stop-motion videos. Users will recognize this popular photo technique from many commercials and the opening credits of popular shows. It can create interesting and even spooky video effects by isolating some parts of the frame to focus and creating more distance between objects and backgrounds in the image.

Monsters Socks ($2.99): This app is an interactive storybook where children help a small monster navigate through several scenes—a neighborhood, the surface of the moon—to find its socks. Cute story, nongrating music, and sympathetic character art make this story and game attractive to children.

Moon Globe HD (free): An interactive globe that rotates, spins, and zooms in and out seamlessly. Turn on/off filters to show spacecraft landing sites with year or geographical name, and move the light of the sun over the moon to create any phase.

NASA App HD (free): A content-rich app presenting thousands of images from NASA telescopes and satellites, live streams from NASA TV, information on current missions,

International Space Station tracker, and reference material about the solar system and space exploration.

NASA Visualization Explorer (free): This app is essentially a news feed of consumer-friendly reporting on advancements in space and climate science. Each story is presented with an informational article and right images, videos, or animations that demonstrate and explain the science at work.

Pages ($9.99): iOS's word processing program is simple and intuitive for users of Microsoft Word, and this app can open and save files in Word (.doc) format. Composing lengthy texts on the iPad's keyboard is challenging, and although this productivity app is useful and powerful, it is not as easy as using a keyboard.

Pandora (free): This Internet radio app from the Music Genome project identifies similar songs and artists to ones users select and then streams them; users can hit the thumbs up or thumbs down on tracks to modify the algorithm for what their stations will play.

PBS (free): This app delivers Public Broadcasting Service programming, from primetime content to archived and special segments, including *Nova* science documentaries, *Frontline*'s investigative journalism, and *Masterpiece*.

Piano (free): This piano emulator is a delightful way to show off the iPad to a new group; try setting multiple iPads side by side running this app until you can see the full run of piano keys at the same time.

PicStitch (free): This app effortlessly makes picture collages with custom frame layouts and basic image editing options inside the app. Users can experiment with fractal images by making several collages and then importing them back into the app to make an even more complicated collage image.

Planets (free): This map of the stars shows locations of planets and constellations, in either a 2D or 3D map, and tracks when which planets are visible from Earth; the 3D map helps young observers orient themselves when observing the night sky and easily see constellations.

Pollution App (free): This app uses the onboard GPS to show users sources of potential air, water, and radio-wave pollution in particular locations. Users can set a custom radius around their location, or search for other locations around the country. Geolocated map data shows the potential source of pollution, as well as current information with the name and address of the corporation or other source of the pollution. Note that this app is optimized for the iPhone screen, so iPad users will use it at half size, or double the image size at a loss of resolution.

PS Express (free): The PS in this app stands for Photoshop, and although this tool is not as powerful as either the professional Creative Suite from Adobe or the home product, Photoshop Elements, it does have many basic image editing options and image tools.

Qwiki (free): This is a reference app with very engaging, photo-heavy interface for ready reference. The following categories are accessible on the interface: News, Local information, Popular, Actors, Cities, Natural Wonders, and Monuments. But the app has many more topics. This is not an in-depth or necessarily authoritative reference source, but is great for ready reference beyond Wikipedia.

Science Glossary (free): This app offers a somewhat limited list of scientific words and definitions. Because this glossary is specifically meant for elementary and high school science classes, many other common scientific terms are missing.

ScreenChomp (free): A screen capture tool that records a video of however users interact with the simple whiteboard; great way to record a simple tutorial for a math or language arts problem.

Singing Fingers (free): A finger-painting app that also records whatever you say (or sing!) while you "paint" in multicolored dots on the screen. When you are done painting, you can press and hold anywhere on the drawing and hear whatever you or your child was singing and saying.

SlideShark (free): An app that opens plays presentations in a variety of formats, including Microsoft PowerPoint, so you can show any presentation with the flexibility of an iPad interface instead of projected on the wall.

Smithsonian Channel (free): This app delivers hundreds of hours of high-quality science, nature, and history programming from the Smithsonian Channel. Excellent informational and multimedia content to support science and nature programming and instruction, as well as fine examples of video production to use as samples in video programs.

Snapseed ($4.99): The price is worth it for this powerful photography and image editing software that has nearly all of the advanced features users might expect from Adobe's Photoshop in an intuitive, easy-to-use tablet interface.

Splice (free): A no-frills but powerful video editing tool that is an excellent alternative to iMovie. Users can shoot video, import and cut it up, add music via in-app purchase or import from iTunes.

Spotify (free): This app streams millions of songs. Users can easily search for an album, artist name, or track name and then listen live. This app helps share music and songs with friends, and is a great way to find new artists to listen to.

Stitcher Radio (free): This app allows users to find any audio—music or talk radio, podcast or performance—and to listen to it on demand. Listen to particular (and local) stations, search for particular episodes of Internet-only broadcasts, and use the embedded social media tools to crowd source your way to your next favorite show.

Storykit (free): An expansive digital storytelling tool that allows users to compose text and lay it out along with images in electronic storybooks, as well as to draw directly on the screen and add recorded music, voice-over, or other sounds. Includes public-domain versions of "The Three Bears" and "The Three Little Pigs" for sample and for remixing.

Storylines (free): A guessing game that combines two kinds of literacy, guessing a word or phrase from a drawing, and then turning that phrase back into another drawing for the next player. Adaptable for at least 2 and up to 12 participants. (A cross between Pictionary and Telephone).

Strip Designer ($2.99): This app is a series of comic strip or graphic novel panel layouts into which users can import photos or drawings, add text boxes and other art, and stickers that say things like "Boom!" and "Pow!"

Tap Quiz Maps (free): This learning quiz app asks users to identify states and provinces of the United States and Canada, and countries around the world, on blank maps.

Teach Me: Kindergarten ($0.99): An app for four- and five-year-olds that presents some key educational content for kindergarten preparation, including sight words, addition, subtraction, and spelling. Users earn rewards for correct answers to questions in a variety of interactive "quests" to learn these four skills.

Tinytap (free): Using any photos, easily create games for toddlers where they have to touch or a tap a specific part of the photo when prompted by voice prompts you record.

Toontastic (free): Choose from various characters and backgrounds and create your own cartoon. Walks users through classic plot structure with five scenes.

UN Country Stats (free): This app is a great alternative to the web-based CIA World Factbook, which is clunky in the iPad browser. Complete sets of geographic, political, and other statistical data are available for hundreds of countries and territories around the world.

U.S. Citizenship (free): Offers study questions and a practice quiz for users studying for the U.S. Citizenship test; choose this app because it offers the questions in Spanish and Chinese as well as in English.

Vestas Weather (free): This app geolocates real-time weather data on a searchable map interface. Use it to compare weather or climate across different parts of the country or world.

VideoScience (free): Eighty videos of hands-on science experiments allow users to virtually experiment without lab or otherwise specialized equipment; topics are appropriate for middle school and up, with many advanced concepts and some popular topics such as "green" plastic, 3D modeling, and air cannons.

Video Star (free): With this music video production app, users can select a song from their iTunes library and instantly start filming their own version of the music video. Some included effects and others available for in-app purchase.

VoiceThread (free): This app is customized for collaboration and allows users to add text or audio annotations to images or slideshows. After users have added annotations, they can share links to the newly created voice thread via email and then add their own annotations to voice threads created by others.

Wattpad (free): An eReader, eBook, and eText service all in one, connecting users to free novels and stories in a variety of genres and categories, including fantasy, romance, mystery, and teen fiction. In addition, users can upload their own fiction and become part of the social electronic text community at Wattpad.

WhirlyGlobe (free): This app is an interactive world globe perfect for use with younger children, because it does not have the level of granular detail most users are used to from Google Earth. Users can zoom into the country/continent level, and tap the screen to turn on country or U.S. state name labels. It spins in any direction, and the display is liquid and attractive to children.

Appendix B

85 Essential Apps for Library Programming (Grouped by Subject)

Note: This list contains the apps described in the preceding pages, as well as others useful in a library setting.

ART

123DSCULPT (free): A 3D sculpture and design app that gives users a lump of virtual clay or several premade shapes to alter. Users can rotate the view in all directions and can interact with the virtual clay much as they would with actual modeling clay.

7 Billion ($4.99): Published by the National Geographic Society, this app features photography, informational text, interactive maps, videos and more all about the impact of a rising human population on Earth. Use these high-quality images to illustrate or inspire research projects and for sparking groups discussions.

Design Museum (free): Digital museum of objects from the collections of the Design Museum of London, presented in a slick and liquid interface that is, itself, as innovative as some of the art on display. Each object in this digital collection has a complete catalog record with detailed information.

DoodleBuddy (free): Simple paint app with preset backgrounds, stamps, and stencils to make more powerful images; contains tools to draw circles and squares.

The Getty Art in L.A. HD (free): This app tells the story of the history of art in Los Angeles from 1945 to 1980, and is made up of four different digital exhibitions. Users can listen to audio content and see painting, photographs, sculpture and other art presented in an information-rich environment.

Getty Images (free): A catalog of stock photos that make excellent writing prompts and illustrations; users can search, browse, save and share some 24 million photos, as claimed by the app. Shake the iPad for a random picture

The Louvre HD (free): A digital subset of the Louvre's iconic collections, accompanied by short informational articles about the painting.

DIGITAL STORYTELLING

Felt Board ($2.99): Create compelling felt scenes with pre-designed characters and shapes. Keep interactive for one-on-one play or use it to create visuals for a digital storytime, which can be shared via the in-app screenshot tool. Colors are bright and attractive, and the art emulates the texture of real felt.

i Tell a Story ($0.99): An easy-to-use podcasting tool that allows users to record audio of any kind and enhance it with sound effects on a simple three-track mixing deck.

Keynote ($9.99): iOS's answer to Microsoft PowerPoint is easy to use and comes with built-in animations and transitions that spice up presentations. Keynote can open and export Power-Point (.ppt) format files as well. The multitouch interface is well suited for presentation making, and this app can be easier to use than a mouse-and-keyboard desktop version.

Miniatures (free): This video tool creates tilt-shift stop-motion videos. Users will recognize this popular photo technique from many commercials and the opening credits of popular shows. It can create interesting and even spooky video effects by isolating some parts of the frame to focus and creating more distance between objects and backgrounds in the image.

Storykit (free): An expansive digital storytelling tool that allows users to compose text and lay it out along with images in electronic storybooks, as well as to draw directly on the screen and add recorded music, voiceover or other sounds. Includes public-domain versions of "The Three Bears" and "The Three Little Pigs" for sample and for remixing.

Strip Designer ($2.99): This app is a series of comic strip or graphic novel panel layouts into which users can import photos or drawings, add text boxes and other art, and stickers that say things like "Boom!" and "Pow!"

Toontastic (free): Choose from various characters and backgrounds and create your own cartoon. It walks users through classic plot structure with five scenes.

VoiceThread (free): this app is customized for collaboration, and allows users to add text or audio annotations to images or slideshows. After users have added annotations, they can share links to the newly created voice thread via email and then add their own annotations to voice threads created by others.

Wattpad (free): An eReader, eBook, and eText service all in one, connecting users to free novels and stories in a variety of genres and categories, including fantasy, romance, mystery and teen fiction. In addition, users can upload their own fiction and become part of the social electronic text community at Wattpad.

EARLY LITERACY

Letters A to Z ($0.99): An app designed for very young children to practice their letter knowledge and phonological awareness skills; users tap a letter to hear its name and tap pictures of objects that animate and play the sound of the letter.

Letter Tracer ($0.99) This simple app is based on a Montessori technique for children to practice writing letters. There are options that allow children to trace an outlined letter and also copy the letter without the tracing guide.

Literacy Skills Sampler HD (free): This app is designed for adults who wish to improve their functional literacy skills. Short videos isolate and highlight basic words, using lots of visuals. Design is bright and clear without being childish or simplistic.

Monsters Socks ($2.99): This app is an interactive storybook where children help a small monster navigate through several scenes—a neighborhood, the surface of the moon—to find its socks. Cute story, nongrating music, and sympathetic character art make this story and game attractive to children.

Singing Fingers (free): A finger-painting app that also records whatever you say (or sing!) while you "paint" in multicolored dots on the screen. When you are done painting, you can press and hold anywhere on the drawing and hear whatever you or your child was singing and saying.

Teach Me: Kindergarten ($0.99): An app for four- and five-year-olds that presents some key educational content for kindergarten preparation, including sight words, addition, subtraction, and spelling. Users earn rewards for correct answers to questions in a variety of interactive "quests" to learn these four skills.

GAMES

CutTheRope ($0.99): This app is an educational game incorporating principles of physics in a dynamic and interactive play space. Users move through a series of challenges in which the goal is getting a cookie in a frog's mouth, and they must conceptualize and experiment with force, velocity, direction, gravity, etc. It takes a very long time for children and young teens to tire of this game!

Jurassic Park (free): This dinosaur-keeping game features simple graphics; users feed, water, and build enclosures as they manage a dinosaur zoo. Similar to iBloom in concept.

Lego 4+ (free): This app is a simple driving game constructed in the style of a classic progressive landscape video game like the original Mario Brothers. Users must first tap together different Lego parts to create more complicated Lego vehicles, which they then use in the game to collect coins as they drive along the landscape. There are also puzzle levels with more complicated Lego objects and scenes to construct.

Storylines (free): A guessing game that combines two kinds of literacy, guessing a word or phrase from a drawing, and then turning that phrase back into another drawing for the next player. Adaptable for at least 2 and up to 12 participants. (A cross between Pictionary and Telephone).

Tinytap (free): Using any photos, easily create games for toddlers where they have to touch or a tap a specific part of the photo when prompted by voice prompts you record.

GEOGRAPHY

Google Earth (free): Google's powerful mapping and satellite imaging data are at your fingertips in this app; includes 3D recreations of some cities as well as views inside famous buildings and landmarks. This is a must-have reference app.

MapBox (free): A powerful mapping tool that draws on many open-source products to provide sophisticated map making, viewing, and sharing capabilities.

Qwiki (free): This is a reference app with very engaging, photo-heavy interface for ready reference. The following categories are accessible on the interface: News, Local information,

Popular, Actors, Cities, Natural Wonders, and Monuments. But the app has many more topics. This is not an in-depth or necessarily authoritative reference source, but is great for ready reference beyond Wikipedia.

Tap Quiz Maps (free): This learning quiz app asks users to identify states and provinces of the United States and Canada, and countries around the world, on blank maps.

UN Country Stats (free): This app is a great alternative to the web-based CIA World Factbook, which is clunky in the iPad browser. Complete sets of geographic, political and other statistical data are available for hundreds of countries and territories around the world.

WhirlyGlobe (free): this app is an interactive world globe perfect for use with younger children, because it does not have the level of granular detail most users are used to from Google Earth. Users can zoom into the country/continent level, and tap the screen to turn on country or U.S. state name labels. It spins in any direction, and the display is liquid and attractive to children.

MUSIC

GarageBand ($4.99): Apple's proprietary music creation app; powerful virtual instrument emulators and mixing capabilities.

Pandora (free): This Internet radio app from the Music Genome project identifies similar songs and artists to ones users select and then streams them; users can hit the thumbs up or thumbs down on tracks to modify the algorithm for what their stations will play.

Piano (free): This piano emulator is a delightful way to show off the iPad to a new group; try setting multiple iPads side by side running this app until you can see the full run of piano keys at the same time.

Spotify (free): This app streams millions of songs. Users can easily search for an album, artist name, or track name and then listen live. This app helps share music and songs with friends, and is a great way to find new artists to listen to.

Stitcher Radio (free): This app allows users to find any audio—music or talk radio, podcast or performance—and to listen to it on demand. Listen to particular (and local) stations, search for particular episodes of Internet-only broadcasts, and use the embedded social media tools to crowd source your way to your next favorite show.

Video Star (free): With this music video production app, users can select a song from their iTunes library and instantly start filming their own version of the music video. Some included effects and others available for in-app purchase.

NEWS

AP Mobile (free): this app delivers breaking news content from the Associated Press. Users can search for particular stories or themes, or see headline news in several categories. Contains text and photo content.

BBC News (free): Delivering international news from the British Broadcasting Company (BBC) in text, audio, and video formats, this app connects users to many kinds of world news.

PHOTO AND IMAGE EDITING

Crayola LCC (Lights, Camera, Color!) ($1.99): This app creates a digital coloring page by draining any photograph of color but maintaining the lines. It has an in-app camera, or users can upload from the photo roll to quickly remove the color from any image, and then color it on the screen with virtual crayons, markers, or pencils.

Fotobabble (free): This app allows users to add voice-over content or text content to one image or a series of images. Use it to create a narrated slideshow or a talking postcard you can email.

LEGO Photo (free): An easy-to-use photo app that turns any image into a photo mosaic that looks like it is made of Legos. Users can tap their mosaic to change to different color schemes.

Loopcam (free): This app is a photo and camera tool that allows users to take up to 50 still photos, which the app then animates into a loop. Great for making popular animated GIFs for Tumblr or sharing on other social network services.

PicStitch (free): This app effortlessly makes picture collages with custom frame layouts and basic image editing options inside the app. Users can experiment with fractal images by making several collages and then importing them back into the app to make an even more complicated collage image.

PS Express (free): The PS in this app stands for Photoshop, and although this tool is not as powerful as either the professional Creative Suite from Adobe or the home product, Photoshop Elements, it does have many basic image editing options and image tools.

Snapseed ($4.99): The price is worth it for this powerful photography and image editing software that has nearly all of the advanced features users might expect from Adobe's Photoshop in an intuitive, easy-to-use tablet interface.

SCIENCE–EARTH SCIENCES AND ASTRONOMY

Arctic Watch (free): This app is powered by NASA satellite data that shows the yearly seasonal ice melt at the Arctic and Antarctic; historical data shows up to 30 years of ice data for comparison.

EarthObserver ($0.99): This app, developed at Columbia University, feeds many kinds of earth science and climate data onto interactive maps of Earth from a variety of governmental and scientific sources, including NASA, USGS, and others. Practice geolocation of data, compare climate data in different parts of the world, and use this app for excellent examples of enhanced maps.

Mars Globe (free): An interactive globe that rotates, spins, and zooms to and from the surface of Mars seamlessly; follow a guided tour or visit over 1,500 geographical features on your own with links to more information.

Moon Globe HD (free): An interactive globe that rotates, spins, and zooms in and out seamlessly. Turn on/off filters to show spacecraft landing sites with year or geographical name, and move the light of the sun over the moon to create any phase.

NASA App HD (free): A content-rich app presenting thousands of images from NASA telescopes and satellites, live streams from NASA TV, information on current missions, International Space Station tracker, and reference material about the solar system and space exploration.

NASA Visualization Explorer (free): This app is essentially a news feed of consumer-friendly reporting on advancements in space and climate science. Each story is presented with an informational article and right images, videos or animations that demonstrate and explain the science at work.

Planets (free): This map of the starts shows locations of planets and constellations in either a 2D or 3D map, and tracks when which planets are visible from Earth; the 3D map helps young observers orient themselves when observing the night sky and easily see constellations.

Vestas Weather (free): This app geolocates real-time weather data on a searchable map interface. Use it to compare weather or climate across different parts of the country or world.

VideoScience (free): Eighty videos of hands-on science experiments allow users to virtually experiment without lab or otherwise specialized equipment; topics are appropriate for middle school and up, with many advanced concepts and some popular topics such as "green" plastic, 3D modeling, and air cannons.

SCIENCE-GENERAL

3D CellStain (free): A set of interactive graphics and microscope photography that display and show the structure and parts of a cell.

BoboExploresLight ($4.99): An interactive science textbook with stunning illustrations that follow a little creature, Bobo, through experiences about the science of light, such as photosynthesis, color, and so on.

Creatures of Light (free): Reference app from the American Museum of Natural History about kinds of bioluminescence, how it works, and how bioluminescent organisms are studied. The text is fairly dense, explaining scientific concepts at levels appropriate for middle schoolers and above, but also has lots of engaging and vivid photographs.

Greenpeace Images (free): Beautiful and high-interest photography of nature from an environmentalist organization; often updated content brings world from the rainforest to the Antarctic, as they advertise, to the iPad.

Exploriments: Electrostatics–Coulomb's Law ($2.99): Interactive electricity experiments with clear illustrations.

Exploriments: Fluids–Archimedes Principle, Buoyancy and Flotation ($3.99): Interactive science experiments about fluid science.

Exploriments: Weight, Mass and Force of Gravity–Effect of Altitude and Comparison across Multiple Planets (free): Six interactive science experiments about weight, mass, and gravity.

iBloom (free): Users grow a virtual flower or virtual vegetable plant in this app, which includes interactive motions to supply the plants with their basic needs: food, water, and air. For example, users blow into the microphone to give their plant air.

LeafSnap HD (free): This ultimate electronic field guide is used to identify trees by photographing their leaves; users take a photograph and then work through the database to match it to a species.

PBS (free): This app delivers Public Broadcasting Service programming, from primetime content to archived and special segments, including *Nova* science documentaries, *Frontline*'s investigative journalism, and *Masterpiece*.

Pollution App (free): This app uses the onboard GPS to show users sources of potential air, water and radio-wave pollution in particular locations. Users can set a custom radius around their location, or search for other locations around the country. Geolocated map data shows the potential source of pollution, as well as current information with the name and address of the corporation or other source of the pollution. Note that this app is optimized for the iPhone screen, so iPad users will use it at half size, or double the image size at a loss of resolution.

Science Glossary (free): This app offers a somewhat limited list of scientific words and definitions. Because this glossary is specifically meant for elementary and high school science classes, many other common scientific terms are missing.

Smithsonian Channel (free): This app delivers hundreds of hours of high-quality science, nature, and history programming from the Smithsonian Channel. Excellent informational and multimedia content to support science and nature programming and instruction, as well as fine examples of video production to use as samples in video programs.

VIDEO EDITING AND PRODUCTION

iMotion HD (free): Make stop-motion animated films with just a few taps. The in-app settings allow users to control the frame capture speed as well as the playback speed to achieve desired stop motion effects, and the app uses an onlon-skin translucent image option to keep your objects exactly where you mean them to be.

iMovie ($4.99): Apple's proprietary video editing application that brings nearly professional-grade editing functionality to home and educational users. Users can create, edit, and share HD movies.

Splice (free): A no-frills but powerful video editing tool that is an excellent alternative to iMovie. Users can shoot video, import and cut it up, add music via in-app purchase or import from iTunes.

MISCELLANEOUS APPS AND UTILITIES

Dropbox (free): Seamlessly share photos, documents and other files between the iPad and any other computer or device; set up public folders to share large files too big to email.

Educreations Interactive Whiteboard (free): A digital whiteboard for working out problems that includes a text tool and 10 different colored markers to choose from.

Epicurious (free): This app is compendium of easy-to-follow recipes with rich photographs and options to search by cuisine or ingredient.

Flipboard (free): Curate your own iPad magazine with this app; pull in content from your social media feeds or from other blogs and magazines to create a digital magazine with custom content.

iTranslate Voice ($0.99): This app is a translation machine to and from 24 major world languages and their dialects; speak into the microphone and the software translates, and it speaks back a reply. Users can also correct the input by using the in-app keyboard.

Job Aware (free): Although this app is primarily a tool to search for job ads, it also comes with helpful content about writing resumes, researching companies, and effective interviewing, as well as offering a salary comparison tool across 50 U.S. cities.

Kindle (free): Amazon's proprietary ereading app, which allows users to download and read Kindle format books (.azw and .KF8). While most of the content is paid, the app is free and any libraries using OverDrive's eBook service will have access to Kindle format books. In addition, Amazon does some free content, especially previews, available to experience.

Merriam Webster Dictionary (free): This is an easy-to-use and authoritative dictionary that offers pronunciation help and synonyms and antonyms in addition to definitions.

Pages ($9.99): iOS's word processing program is simple and intuitive for users of Microsoft Word, and this app can open and save files in Word (.doc) format. Composing lengthy texts on the iPad's keyboard is challenging, and although this productivity app is useful and powerful, it is not as easy as using a keyboard.

ScreenChomp (free): A screen capture tool that records a video of however users interact with the simple whiteboard; great way to record a simple tutorial for a math or language arts problem.

SlideShark (free): An app that opens plays presentations in a variety of formats, including Microsoft PowerPoint, so you can show any presentation with the flexibility of an iPad interface instead of projected on the wall.

U.S. Citizenship (free): Offers study questions and a practice quiz for users studying for the U.S. Citizenship test; choose this app because it offers the questions in Spanish and Chinese as well as in English.

Index

About the Author

JOEL A. NICHOLS is a branch manager and children's librarian at the Free Library of Philadelphia. He has also worked as a digital resources supervisor and instructor aboard the Free Library Techmobile, adult/teen services librarian, and has taught college English. He has an MSLIS from Drexel University, an MA in Creative Writing from Temple University, and an honors BA in German from Wesleyan University. He also studied at the Humboldt-Universitaet in Berlin, Germany, supported by a Fulbright.